Nature, Human Nature, and God

Nature,
Human Nature,
and God

Ian G. Barbour

FORTRESS PRESS
Minneapolis

Nature, Human Nature, and God

ISBN: 0-8006-3477-2

Manufactured in the U.S.A.

06   05   04   03   02   1   2   3   4   5   6   7   8   9   10

Contents

Preface

Current scientific theories present five challenges to religious thought today.

- Is belief in a personal God compatible with the scientific account of evolution? How could God act in nature if evolutionary history is the product of random mutations and natural selection?
- Are we determined by our genes, inherited from more primitive ancestors? Does evolutionary science require us to reject or revise the traditional Christian understanding of human nature? What ethical norms can guide the applications of genetics such as genetic modification, cloning, or stem-cell research?
- Does neuroscience (the study of the brain) show that all mental activity is determined by the interaction of neurons? If intelligence is the capacity to process information, can we expect that the artificial intelligence of robots will surpass all human capacities? Is the traditional idea of the human soul defensible today?
- Is the classical view of divine omnipotence compatible with a law-abiding world and with the existence of evil, suffering, and human freedom? Or do recent portrayals of God's self-limitation allow us to think of God's power as the empowerment of other beings rather than as unilateral power over them?
- Has the separation of God and nature and the sharp distinction between humanity and other creatures in the history of Christian thought contributed to the current environmental crisis? How might the biblical concern for social justice be expressed in relation to the global environmental and social impacts of technology today?

In this volume I take these questions up in successive chapters, following an Introduction that sets forth the general approach of the book as a whole. Behind these particular questions lies a more fundamental one. Can we reformulate aspects of the traditional understanding of God, nature, and human nature in the light of science while preserving the central message of the gospel?

Earlier versions of two of these chapters were given as presentations to conferences organized by the Vatican Observatory and the Center for Theology and the Natural Sciences (CTNS) in Berkeley, California. I am enduringly grateful to CTNS and to the vision and initiative of its founder and director, Robert John Russell. For more than two decades CTNS has pursued a pioneering program of conferences, publications, and education. It has offered courses to seminary, master's and doctoral students as a member of the Graduate Theological Union, and it has enlisted the active participation of outstanding scientists from across the United States and overseas. I know of no other center in the world that is making such a significant contribution to the creative dialogue between science and religion.

1

Introduction

Four views of the relation of science and religion are widely held today: conflict, independence, dialogue, and integration.

(1) *Conflict.* Biblical literalists believe that the theory of evolution conflicts with religious faith. Atheistic scientists defend a philosophy of materialism and argue that evolution is incompatible with any form of theism. For both groups science and religion are enemies. This view receives most of the attention in the media, since conflict makes a more exciting news story than the distinctions made by the scientists and theologians who believe both in God and in evolution.

(2) *Independence.* Conflict can be avoided if science and religion are kept in separate compartments of human life. Science and religion deal with differing domains and contrasting aspects of reality. Science asks how things work and relies on objective public data. Religion asks about values and a larger framework of meaning for personal life. In this view, the two forms of discourse do not compete because they serve completely different functions. The two kinds of inquiry offer complementary perspectives on the world that are not mutually exclusive. Compartmentalization avoids conflict but at the price of preventing any constructive interaction.

(3) *Dialogue.* One form of dialogue is a comparison of the methods of the two fields, which may show similarities even when the differences are acknowledged. For example, conceptual models and analogies are used to imagine what cannot be directly observed (God or a quark, for example). Dialogue may also occur when science raises questions at its boundaries that it cannot itself answer, such as: why is there a universe at all, and why is it orderly and intelligible? In addition, even if science and

religion are relatively independent, there may be interesting analogies between particular concepts in the two fields.

(4) *Integration.* Some people seek a more systematic integration of science and religion. Those in the tradition of *natural theology* hope to find in science a proof (or at least suggestive evidence) of the existence of God. Other people start from a particular religious tradition and argue that many of its beliefs are compatible with modern science but some beliefs should be reformulated in the light of particular scientific theories. I call such an approach *a theology of nature* (within a religious tradition) rather than a natural theology (arguing from science alone). Some versions of a theology of nature make use of an integrated philosophy, such as *process philosophy,* which systematically elaborates a set of concepts relevant to both science and religion.

In my recent book, *When Science Meets Religion,* I used this fourfold typology in each of the chapters to explore the theological implications of particular scientific fields: astronomy, quantum physics, evolutionary biology, and genetics and neuroscience.[1] In the present volume I restrict myself to the last of the four types, *Integration,* which I consider the most promising option. This allows me to spend more time developing my own views and less time trying to survey the field or offering criticism of views with which I disagree.

I discuss here the theological implications of the biological sciences: evolution, genetics, neuroscience, and ecology. I have elsewhere given attention to the physical sciences: astronomy, quantum physics, thermodynamics, and relativity.[2] I also explore here some ethical questions arising from genetic engineering (chapter 3) and the global environmental crisis (chapter 6). In some of my writings I have considered the application of the fourfold typology to other religious traditions, but here I confine myself to the Christian tradition, with which I am most familiar.

Recent years have seen a revival of interest in natural theology. In the early nineteenth century the argument from design was popular and persuasive when it was widely assumed that an essentially unchanging universe had been created all at once. The argument for the specific design of every creature in its present form was undermined by Charles Darwin's theory of natural selection. Darwin himself, however, accepted a revised version of the argument, holding that the long process by which evolution had occurred was itself designed by God. Some astronomers now assert that the physical constants of the early universe seem to be fine-tuned for the existence of life. If the expansion rate a second after the Big Bang 14 billion years ago had been even a tiny fraction greater or smaller, the universe would have dispersed or collapsed too rapidly for the formation of galaxies, planets, life, and intelligence.

More skeptical astronomers suggest that perhaps there are many universes with differing physical constants and we just happen by chance to live in one with parameters suitable for life. Successive universes might have followed each other in cycles of expansion and contraction, or separate universes might have originated from quantum fluctuations in a primordial vacuum and continue to exist in parallel with each other. But the idea of multiple universes is highly speculative since the other universes would be in principle unobservable from ours. Moreover, the question of design would arise again at an earlier stage. What explains the structures of space-time and laws of quantum physics that could result in even one world suitable for life and intelligence? These new versions of natural theology are currently being debated by both scientists and theologians. My main objection to them is theological rather than scientific. Even if the argument is accepted, it leads only to the distant God of deism who designed the universe and then left it to run itself—not the God of theism actively involved with the world and human life.

Instead of starting from science, as natural theology does, a *theology of nature* starts from a religious tradition based on the religious experience of a historical community. Advocates of this approach hold that some traditional doctrines—especially doctrines of God and human nature—need to be reformulated in the light of current science. Theological doctrines must be consistent with the scientific evidence, even if they are not derivable from current scientific theories.

Throughout most of Christian history the cosmos was thought to be an essentially static and unchanging order. Today nature is known to be a dynamic evolutionary process with a long history of emergent novelty, characterized throughout by both law and chance. The natural order is ecological, interdependent, and multileveled. These characteristics will modify our representation of the relation of both God and humanity to nonhuman nature. This will, in turn, affect our attitudes toward nature and will have practical implications for environmental ethics. The problem of evil will also be viewed very differently in an evolutionary rather than a static world.

In the task of theological reformulation, I believe that we should take the Bible seriously but not literally. Starting in the nineteenth century, biblical scholars used historical methods to study the cultural contexts in which various parts of the Bible were written. They noted that the creation stories in Genesis made significant affirmations that the world is good, orderly, and dependent on a purposeful God. These religious convictions were conveyed through a symbolic and poetic story that assumed the prescientific cosmology of its day, which included a seven-day creation, an earth-centered astronomy, and a three-deck universe with heaven above and hell below our world. But the religious message of Genesis can be accepted today because it is not dependent on its ancient cosmology, and it is also quite independent of modern scientific cosmology. Its message is not really about events in the past but about the fundamental relation of God to the world and to us in every moment. In an evolutionary world we must give attention to continuing creation rather than to events in the distant past. Our task is to try to express the central message of the gospel in contemporary terms.

The traditional view held that the first humans, Adam and Eve, were created in the garden of Eden. According to this view, Adam disobeyed God and as punishment he was expelled from the garden. Death and suffering entered the world. All subsequent human beings inherited original sin from which they can be saved only by the merits of Christ's death. However, the evolutionary account says that there never was a paradise without conflict, death, and suffering, and that we are descendants of earlier prehuman forms. Part of our task, then, is to reinterpret the idea of original sin and redemption within an evolutionary understanding of our past.

I believe that revelation occurred, not in the dictation of an infallible book, but in the lives of people. The Bible is the human record of divine initiative and human response, first in the Hebrew prophets and the Israelite community and then in the life of Christ and the early church. Theology is critical reflection on these scriptural documents and the ongoing experience of the worshipping community. But the concepts in which theology is expressed are inescapably influenced by cultural assumptions, such as the Hellenistic ideas of the early church fathers, the Aristotelian philosophy of the Middle Ages, or the scientific world of today. The view of revelation defended here would allow for divine initiative and interpretive response in other religious traditions—and on other planets, if intelligent life exists elsewhere in the universe.

While I accept the evidence for evolution, as almost all scientists do, I do not accept the philosophy of *materialism* that is assumed or defended by many scientists. Materialism is the assertion that matter is the fundamental reality in the universe. Materialism is a form of *metaphysics* (a set of claims concerning the most general characteristics and constituents of reality). It is often accompanied by a second assertion: the scientific method is the only reliable path to knowledge. This is a form of *epistemology* (a set of claims concerning inquiry and the acquisition of knowledge). The two assertions are linked: if the only real entities are those with which science deals, then science is the only valid path to knowledge.

In addition, many forms of materialism express *reductionism*. Epistemological reductionism claims that the laws and theories of all the sciences are in principle reducible to the laws of physics and chemistry. Metaphysical reductionism claims that the component parts of any system determine its behavior. The materialist believes that all phenomena will eventually be explained in terms of the actions of material components, which are the only effective causes in the world. In the past, powerful new theories excited the imagination of scientists who sometimes extrapolated them beyond their proper domains. In the eighteenth century many scientists thought that Newtonian physics could in principle account for all phenomena, but in the twentieth century quantum physics has shown the limits of such predictability. Today molecular biology is an immensely fruitful research program, and we may be tempted to think that it will explain the behavior of all living things. But new ideas in the biological sciences encourage a less reductionist view.

Scientists have often extended scientific concepts beyond their scientific use to support comprehensive *materialistic philosophies*. The identification of the real with measurable properties that can be correlated by exact mathematical relationships started in the physical sciences, but it influenced scientists in other fields and continues today. I would argue that the quantifiable properties of matter have been abstracted from the real world by ignoring the particularity of events and the nonquantifiable aspects of human experience. We do not have to conclude that matter alone is real or that mind, purpose, and human love are only byproducts of matter in motion.

In their popular writings, scientists tend to invoke the authority of science for ideas that are not really part of science itself. Theism and materialism are alternative belief systems, each claiming to encompass all reality. If science is taken to be the only acceptable form of understanding, then explanation in terms of evolutionary history, biochemical mechanisms, or scientific theories excludes all other forms of explanation. I suggest that the concept of God is not a hypothesis formulated to explain the relation between particular events in the world in competition with scientific hypotheses. Belief in God is primarily a commitment to a way of life in response to distinctive kinds of religious experience in communities formed by historic traditions; it is not a substitute for scientific research. Religious beliefs offer a wider framework of meaning in which particular events can be contextualized.

As an alternative to reductionism I will defend *holism,* the thesis that the behavior of a system affects the behavior of its parts. In addition to the bottom-up causal influence of parts on integrated wholes, wholes exert a top-down influence on their component parts—not in violation of lower-level laws but by setting boundary conditions for those laws. Holism is already evident in physics in nonlocal phenomena such as the correlation of the properties of two particles that were formed in a single quantum event. Holistic behavior is found in solid-state physics, in the self-organization of complex thermodynamic systems, in the development of an embryo, in the networks studied in systems theory, and, I will suggest, in the mental activities of the brain.

Whereas holism refers to the behavior of an existing system, *emergence* refers to the temporal appearance of novel properties in a system when it is assembled. In some cases the new properties can be predicted from the properties of the previous components and their organization. For example, the wetness of water is not a property of hydrogen and oxygen but it can be predicted from the dynamical laws of the molecules formed when the elements are combined. In other cases, higher-level activities alter the structural organization of the components, as in the development of an embryo. The most complex and unpredictable emergence occurs when information representing a particular state can be repeatedly re-entered in successive cycles to alter existing structures, as in the case of DNA formed in the evolutionary history of organisms in their ongoing interaction with the environment and with other organisms. The behavior of water is quite independent of its previous history, but the behavior of an organism is not because in its history multiple levels of causality are linked across a wide span of space and time.

I have found the *process philosophy* of Alfred North Whitehead and his followers helpful in my attempt to integrate scientific and religious concepts. I have been indebted to the process theologians, especially John Cobb and David Griffin, who use Whitehead's philosophical ideas to interpret the Christian faith without the technical terminology employed by Whitehead himself. While I accept the process critiques of divine omnipotence and of the body/soul dualism of classical Christianity, I defend a stronger assertion of God's power and a more integral view of selfhood than is found in White-head's writing. Because process thought may be unfamiliar to many readers, I develop important process themes in the early sections of each chapter without any specific reference to process philosophy. Only in the concluding section of each chapter do I try to show how process philosophy can integrate these themes in a distinctive way.

Theologians and philosophers bring their own conceptual frameworks to the interpretation of scientific theories. The theologian draws from the experiences, rituals, stories, and beliefs of a historical religious community. The philosopher seeks a coherent view of religious, aesthetic, moral, and cultural, as well as scientific features of human life. We cannot expect even a nonreductionist science to provide a complete or adequate account of human nature because there are so many kinds of activity and levels of organization intermediate between molecules and persons in communities—including the relationships studied by evolutionary biology, neuroscience, cognitive science, developmental and social psychology, anthropology, history, literature, and the arts, as well as religious studies.

Philosophers and theologians can offer scientists wider intellectual and personal contexts for their work, suggestions of ways to relate it to other disciplines, and the analysis of ethical issues arising from scientific theories and their applications. They can also encourage scientists to examine the philosophical assumptions underlying their judgments as to what features of phenomena are important to investigate and what types of concepts might be plausible—without denying that scientific theories must always be judged by the criteria of science: scope, consistency, compatibility with empirical data, and fruitfulness in suggesting further research.

Successive chapters of this volume take up specific topics. God's relation to evolution is discussed in chapter 2. If nature follows exact laws and there are no gaps in which God might intervene, how can we say that evolution is God's way of creating? Can God act at all if events in evolutionary history are determined by random mutation and natural selection? We will note first that Darwinism itself has evolved since Darwin's day. Biologists have described distinctive features of organic life such as self-organization, indeterminacy, top-down causality, and the communication of information. These ideas have led to new concepts of God—as designer of a self-organizing system, as determiner of indeterminacies, as top-down cause, or as communicator of information. Process thought articulates similar ideas but adds the proposal that God acts through the interiority of every organism, especially at its highest level of integration.

Chapter 3 examines the implications of evolution and genetics for our understanding of human nature. Should we accept the claims of sociobiologists that apparent altruism among social insects and human morality today can both be explained by behavior that contributed to the survival of genes in evolutionary history? Does research on chimpanzees showing their ability to learn sign language undermine belief in the uniqueness of humanity? Or do human capacities for symbolic representation, spoken language, and culture set us apart from all other creatures? Evolutionary history suggests the need to reformulate traditional Christian doctrines about humanity as created in God's image, fallen in original sin, and redeemed by Christ. How do studies of the correlation of human behavioral traits with particular genes affect our understanding of human freedom? The chapter also considers ethical issues, such as genetic modification, cloning, and stem-cell research.

Chapter 4 deals with neuroscience, artificial intelligence, and human nature. Neuroscience (the study of the brain) shows that intelligence is embodied, emotional, and inherently social. Many computer experts have identified intelligence with the ability to process information, whether in computer circuits or in the human brain. But recent designs for robots have emphasized embodiment, interaction with the environment, and learning from experience. I will suggest that the idea of an embodied social self in neuroscience and robotics actually accords well with the biblical view, though classical Christianity (drawing largely from Greek thought) adopted a sharp dualism of body and soul that is difficult to reconcile with the scientific evidence today. The status of consciousness remains problematic in both neuroscience and computer science; and philosophical interpretations have included reductive materialism, two-aspect theories, and claims of the irreducibility of consciousness. Process thought holds that there is a mental and a physical aspect in every entity—a subjective interiority as well as an objective causal relation to other entities—though it holds that consciousness occurs only at higher organizational levels in multilevel integrated organisms.

Chapter 5 is a more theological discussion of God's relation to nature. Can we accept today the classical Christian view of divine omnipotence? I will first indicate the diversity of models of God in biblical thought and the dominance of the monarchical model of divine omnipotence in Medieval thought. Then I will note that recent portrayals of God's self-limitation are motivated by recognition of the integrity of nature; the existence of evil, suffering and human freedom; and the Christian understanding of the cross. Feminist authors have also given impressive critiques of patriarchal and monarchical models of God. Process thinkers share these objections to divine omnipotence, though they hold that the limitations of God's power are a feature of the nature of reality, including God's nature, rather than God's voluntary decision. Process thought defends God's ability to empower and nurture other beings rather than to overpower and control them.

In chapter 6 the implications of ecology and theology for environmental ethics are considered. Ecology and other sciences have made us aware of the interdependence of all forms of life, but theology can also encourage new environmental attitudes. Classical Christianity contributed to the environmental crisis by its emphasis on divine transcendence rather than immanence and by the sharp line it drew between humanity and other forms of life. But from the Bible itself we can reclaim neglected themes of stewardship, celebration of nature, the Holy Spirit in nature, and the sacred in nature. From recent theology—especially process theology—we can find new formulations of God's immanence and of our kinship with other creatures. Specific environmental policies also raise questions of social justice. Who benefits and who bears the risks from the environmental and social impacts of technology? Accelerating globalization brings new investment and new technologies to developing nations, but often at the expense of environmental preservation and economic and political self-determination. I will suggest in conclusion that both science and religion can contribute significantly to the building of a more just and sustainable society on planet Earth.

2

God and Evolution

Is evolutionary theory compatible with the idea that God acts in nature? Through most of Western history it had been assumed that all creatures were designed and created by God in their present forms, but Charles Darwin claimed that they are the product of a long process of natural selection. His theory of evolution not only undermined the traditional version of the argument from design; it also explained the history of nature by scientific laws that seemed to offer no opportunity for God's providential guidance. Several themes in the biological sciences, however, offer promising new ways of conceiving of divine action in evolutionary history without intervention in violation of the laws of nature.

The first section of this chapter traces the development of evolutionary theory from Darwin himself to molecular biology and recent hypotheses about complexity. The second explores four themes in recent writing about biological processes: self-organization, indeterminacy, top-down causality, and communication of information. The third section examines theological models of God's action in nature based on analogies with each of these four characteristics of organic life. In the final section I suggest that process theology avoids some of the problems arising in other models of God's relation to nature.

Darwinism Evolving

Evolutionary theory has undergone significant reinterpretation and modification since Darwin. First, the growth of population genetics and molecular biology is briefly described. Then the expansion of Darwinism is discussed, particularly recognition that other factors in addition to natural selection influence the direction of evolutionary change. Finally, recent theories of complexity and self-organization are considered.

1. From Darwin to DNA

In Darwin's day, Newtonian mechanics was looked on as the form of science that other sciences should emulate. The Newtonian viewpoint was atomistic, deterministic, and reductionistic. It was believed that the behavior of all systems is determined by a few simple laws governing the behavior of their smallest components. Change was thought to be the result of external forces, such as gravity, acting on bodies that are themselves essentially passive. Darwin agreed with the philosophers of science who held that Newtonian physics represented an ideal for all the sciences, and his theory of evolution shared many of its assumptions.[1]

Darwin held that evolutionary change is caused by natural selection acting on variations among individual members of a species. Under competitive conditions, those individuals with a slight adaptive advantage will survive better to reproduce and pass on that advantage to their offspring. His viewpoint was "atomistic" in assuming that selection acts on separate traits in individual organisms. For him, as for Isaac Newton, change was the result of external forces; he held that the direction of change is determined by natural selection, not by the efforts of organisms themselves as Jean Baptiste Lamark had believed. The assumptions that Darwin shared with Newton are explored in detail in a recent volume by Depew and Weber.[2]

By the end of the nineteenth century, *probability* was an important concept in several areas of physics. Ludwig Bolzmann showed that the probability of different configurations of gas molecules can be calculated, even when the motions of individual molecules are too complicated to calculate. Statistical averages can be used to predict the relationship between large-scale variables, such as pressure, volume, temperature, heat flow, and entropy. In statistical mechanics and classical thermodynamics, equilibrium macrostates can be calculated without knowing the initial distribution of molecules.

Probabilistic reasoning was also important in the merging of *population genetics* and evolutionary theory early in the twentieth century in the theories of Ronald Fisher, Sewall Wright, and Theodosius Dobzhansky. Fisher acknowledged the influence of nineteenth-century physics on his ideas about calculating gene probabilities in individual organisms and gene frequencies in populations. The *"modern synthesis"* in which Julian Huxley, G. G. Simpson, and Ernst Mayr were prominent, continued the Darwinian belief that the evolution of species was the result of a gradual accumulation of small changes. If some members of a population are geographically or reproductively isolated from other members, accumulated changes may result in a new species that can no longer interbreed with the original population. In a very small isolated population, gene frequencies may differ, purely by chance, from those in the larger population; the direction of evolutionary change ("genetic drift") would then be the result of chance rather than natural selection. But natural selection was still viewed as the principal agent of evolutionary change.[3]

The discovery of *the structure of DNA* in 1953 led to identification of the molecular components of the genes that population genetics had postulated. A gene is now known to be a segment of DNA that provides the information needed to assemble a particular protein. The "central dogma" of molecular biology asserted that information is transferred in one direction only, from the sequences of bases in DNA to the sequences of amino acids assembled by the DNA to form proteins. It was claimed that the environment has no direct effect on genes except to eliminate or perpetuate them through selective pressures on the organisms that carried them. Molecular biology has been immensely fruitful in illuminating almost every aspect of evolutionary history, but some of the assumptions initially associated with it have more recently been questioned.

2. The Expansion of Darwinism

Most of the challenges to the modern synthesis in recent decades should be seen as part of an expanded Darwinism (or neo-Darwinism), rather than as a rejection of earlier insights. For example, it has been claimed that *selection occurs at many levels* and not just on the level of organisms in populations. Dawkins speaks of selection at the level of genes; he views organisms as mechanisms by which genes perpetuate themselves. Edward O. Wilson speaks of kin selection, and others defend group selection. Both philosophers and biologists have argued that selection occurs also at the species level. Whereas an organism produces other organisms by reproduction, and it perishes by death, a species produces other species by speciation, and it perishes by extinction. The speciation rate of a species may be as important in the long run as the reproduction rate of individual organisms. Variation and selection occurs at several levels at once, and of course changes at one level will influence those at other levels.[4] Darwin himself stressed the struggle and competition for survival, but more recent interpretations point to a larger role for cooperation and symbiosis.

The idea of *punctuated equilibrium* defended by Stephen Jay Gould and Niles Eldredge challenged the earlier assumption that macroevolution is the result of the gradual accumulation of many small changes. They point to fossil records that show millions of years with very little change, interspersed with bursts of rapid speciation, especially in the early Cambrian period, when all the known phyla and basic body plans appeared in a relatively short period (on a geological time-scale). They postulate that alterations in developmental sequences produced major structural changes. Their view is *holistic* in directing attention to polygenic traits, the genome as a system, and the role of regulatory programs in development—rather than to small changes due to mutations in single genes governing separate traits that might be subject to selection. The directions of change are determined by the possibilities of developmental reorganization as well as by selective forces acting on organisms.[5]

Gould and Lewontin hold that evolutionary change arises from *many differing causes,* and they criticize explanation by natural selection alone ("panadaptationism"). They point out that one can always postulate a possible "selective advantage" for any trait by making up a "just-so story" of how it might be adaptive, even in the absence of independent evidence for such an advantage.[6] But most biologists probably follow Stebbins and Ayala in claiming that all the known data are consistent with an expanded and enriched version of neo-Darwinism in which variation and natural selection are still the main factors in evolutionary change.[7] The communication of information from DNA to proteins is indeed crucial, as the "central dogma" asserted; but other sources of information are significant in determining how genes are expressed in living organisms. Some of this information is in the cytoplasm outside the cell nucleus, and some comes from elsewhere in the organism or wider environment. A complex feedback and regulatory system turns particular genetic programs on and off. Outside influences can also affect the transposition of genes.[8]

Some biologists have noted that the *internal drives* and novel actions of organisms can initiate evolutionary changes. The environment selects individuals, but individuals also select environments; and in a new niche a different set of genes may contribute to survival. Some pioneering fish ventured onto land and were the ancestors of amphibians and mammals; some mammals later returned to the water and were the ancestors of dolphins and whales; some forest woodpeckers began to hunt in the mountains. In each case organisms themselves took new initiatives; genetic and then anatomic changes followed from their actions through "genetic assimilation" (the Baldwin effect). The changes were not initiated by genetic variations. Lamark was evidently right that the purposeful actions of organisms can eventually lead to physiological changes, though he was wrong in assuming that physiological changes occurring during an organism's lifetime can be inherited directly by its offspring.[9]

Finally, some biologists, including Mayr, Gould, and Lewontin, consider themselves exponents of an expanded Darwinism but insist on *the autonomy of biology* from physics. They say that even the probabilistic physics of classical thermodynamics cannot serve as a model for evolutionary biology because chance and contingent historical contexts play such crucial roles. We can describe evolution through a unique historical narrative, but we cannot deduce its path from predictive laws. These authors also defend the distinctiveness of biological concepts and their irreducibility to the concepts of physics and chemistry, as I will note later.[10]

3. Beyond Darwinism?

Darwin's theory shared many of the assumptions of Newtonian physics; the modern synthesis was influenced by the probabilistic reasoning of statistical mechanics. Future understanding of evolution may be enhanced by recent work on *chaos* and *complexity* in the physical sciences. Whereas the linear systems of classical thermodynamics are insensitive to small initial differences and attain predictable equilibrium states, nonlinear thermodynamic systems far from equilibrium are extremely sensitive to very small initial differences and are therefore unpredictable. Prigogine and others have described the emergence of new types of order in dissipative systems far from equilibrium. An infinitesimal difference in initial conditions will lead to alternative end-states and new levels of order described by system-wide relationships rather than by interactions at the molecular level.[11]

Stuart Kauffman draws from theories of complexity in arguing that evolution is the product of *self-organization* as well as chance and selection. He looks at the common properties of diverse systems, for example those in embryonic development, neural networks, and computer networks. As we will see in the next section, he argues that dynamical systems can achieve new ordered states without any external selective pressures.[12] Jeffrey Wicken has insisted that we cannot understand evolutionary history without looking at the entropy, order, and flow of energy in the wider ecosystems within which organisms co-evolve. Moreover, he says, structural and thermodynamic constraints drastically limit the stable combinations when amino acids are randomly assembled to form proteins. These authors adopt a holistic approach that attempts analysis at a variety of levels, avoiding the reductionism evident in much of evolutionary theory.

They claim that natural selection works on a field of already self-organized systems.[13]

In the past, the phenomena of *embryology* and *developmental biology* have been poorly understood and have been difficult to incorporate into neo-Darwinism. How do cells differentiate so that the right organs are formed at the right place in the growing organism? Some biologists postulated a "morphogenic field" that imposes a pre-existing plan that guides cells in their differentiation. Others postulated "developmental pathways" that direct growth toward specific anatomical forms. These hypotheses appear increasingly dubious in the light of recent research on genetic and molecular mechanisms in embryological development. Regulatory genes produce proteins that act as "switches" to turn on secondary genes, which in turn control the tertiary genes responsible for protein assembly in cells, tissues, and organs. In recent experiments, the master control gene that initiates the program for the development of an eye in the fruit fly was introduced into cells on its wings, legs, and antennae, and complete eyes developed at these sites. If the control gene for eye development in a *mouse* is inserted in cells of a fly's wing, *a fly's eye* will develop—suggesting that the control genes for eyes in the two species are virtually unchanged since a common evolutionary ancestor, even though the eye structures of insects and mammals evolved in radically different directions.[14] Our understanding of such processes is still very limited, but research on the molecular basis of development holds great promise for broadening our understanding of evolutionary history. For example, the Cambrian explosion of new phyla may well have been caused by changes in the genetic networks that regulate very early development.

Even after recognizing the power of molecular explanations, however, one can argue that developmental patterns are constrained by principles of *hierarchical organization* and the possible forms of physiological structures. The variability of phenotypes (body structures) is limited by the architecture and dynamics of developmental systems. Goodwin, Ho, and Saunders have defended a structuralism in which a relatively autonomous developmental dynamics is the main source of macroevolution.[15] These ideas are controversial and outside the mainstream of current biological thought, but they should not be dismissed if they might be able to account for observed phenomena more adequately then neo-Darwinist theory.

These authors see themselves as having moved beyond even an expanded Darwinism. If these ideas prove fruitful they may lead to what Thomas Kuhn would call a *paradigm shift*,[16] in which the basic assumptions of Newtonian and nineteenth-century physics will be replaced by an alternative set of assumptions. Or perhaps we could adopt the terminology of Imre Lakatos and say that the core of Darwinism (the importance of variation and natural selection) will have been preserved by abandoning some of its *auxiliary hypotheses* (such as gradualism and the exclusive role of selection as a directive force). We could also follow the philosophers of science who hold that in studying complex phenomena we should seek *limited models* applicable to particular domains, rather than universally applicable predictive laws. Natural selection may be more important in some contexts than in others. As a minimum we can say that we should consider other factors in addition to variation and natural selection and that we should look at what is going on at a variety of levels. In the discussion that follows, I will be drawing primarily from the advocates of "the expansion of Darwinism," but I will refer to the work of Stuart Kauffman, who considers himself "beyond Darwinism."

Biological Processes

Four concepts in recent biological thought require more careful analysis: self-organization, indeterminacy, top-down causality, and communication of information. Each of these concepts is crucial in one of the theological interpretations explored in the subsequent section.

1. Self-Organization

Evolutionary history does indeed show a *directionality*, a trend toward greater complexity and consciousness. There has been an increase in the genetic information in DNA, and a steady advance in the ability of organisms to gather and process information about the environment and respond to it. The emergence of life, consciousness, and human culture are especially significant transitions within a gradual and continuous process. But evolution does not display any straight-line progressive development. For the majority of species, opportunistic adaptations led to dead ends and extinction when conditions changed. The pattern of evolution does not resemble a uniformly growing tree so much as a sprawling bush whose tangled branches grow in many directions and often die off. Nevertheless there is an overall trend. Who can doubt that a human being represents an astonishing advance over an amoeba or a worm?

Some authors have argued that if the amino acids in primeval oceans had *assembled themselves by chance* to form protein chains, the probability of being assembled in the right order to form a particular protein would be fantastically small. It would be highly unlikely to occur even in spans of time many times longer than the history of the universe.[17] The argument is dubious because amino acids do not combine by chance with equal probability, for there are built-in affinities and bonding preferences and structural possibilities. Some combinations form stable units that persist, and these units combine to form larger units. Organic molecules have a capacity for self-organization and complexity because of structural constraints and potentialities.

Other authors have used *hierarchy theory* to indicate how advances to a higher level of organizational complexity are preserved. Imagine a watchmaker whose work is disrupted occasionally. If he has to start over again each time, he would never finish his task. But if he assembles groups of parts into stable subassemblies, which are then combined, he will finish the task more rapidly. Living organisms have many stable subassemblies at differing levels, which are often preserved intact and only loosely coupled to each other. The higher level of stability often arises from functions that are relatively independent of variations in the microscopic details. Evolution exhibits both *chance* and *directionality* because higher levels embody new types of order and stability that are maintained and passed on.[18]

Let us examine Kauffman's thesis that evolution is a product of *self-organization* as well as of random variation and natural selection. He finds similar patterns in the behavior of complex systems that appear very different—for example, in molecules, cells, neural networks, ecosystems, and technological and economic systems. In each case feedback mechanisms and nonlinear interactions make cooperative activity possible in larger wholes. The systems show similar emergent *systemic* properties not present in their components. Kauffman gives particular attention to the behavior of networks. For example, an array of 100,000 light bulbs, each of which goes on or off as an adjustable function of input from its four neighbors, will cycle through only 327 states from among the astronomical number of possible states. Genes are also connected in networks; in the simplest case, gene A represses gene B and vice versa, so only one of them is turned on. Kauffman notes that there are only 256 cell types in mammals, and suggests that this may be the result of system principles and not merely a historical accident.[19]

Many of Kauffman's ideas are speculative and exploratory, but they reflect a new way of looking at evolution. He finds that *order emerges spontaneously* in complex systems, especially on the border between order and chaos. Too much order makes change impossible; too much chaos makes continuity impossible. We should see ourselves not as a highly improbable historical accident but as an expected fulfillment of the natural order. In his book, *At Home in the Universe,* Kauffman calls for awe and respect for a process in which such self-organization occurs.

2. Indeterminacy

Many features of evolutionary history are the product of *unpredictable events.* The particular pair of organisms that mate and the particular combination of genes that are inherited by their offspring cannot be predicted; genetic laws can only be expressed probabilistically for individuals in large populations. Many mutations and replication errors seem to occur at random. A few individuals may form a small isolated population that happens to differ genetically from the average of the larger population, leading to "genetic drift." Such unpredictability is compounded when co-evolving species interact competitively or cooperatively in historically contingent ecosystems and environments. An asteroid collision at the end of the Permian period may have drastically altered the earth's climate and its evolutionary history. We can only describe evolution by a historical narrative; we could not have predicted its course.

Many of these "chance events" seem to represent the unpredictable *intersection of separate causal chains.* Two causal chains may each be determinate, but if they are completely independent of each other, no lawful regularity describes their intersection in time and space. The idea of a causal chain is of course an abstraction. When we speak of "the cause" of an event we are selecting from among the many necessary and jointly sufficient conditions the one to which we want to direct attention in a particular context of inquiry. But our ignorance of the immensely complicated and ramifying web of causal influences in evolutionary history does not in itself imply that it is not determined.

But an indeterminacy in nature itself seems to be present *at the quantum level.* In quantum theory, predictions of individual events among atoms and subatomic particles give only probabilities and not exact values. A particular radioactive atom might decay in the next second or a thousand years from now, and the theory does not tell us which will occur. Some physicists think that this unpredictability is attributable to the limitations of current theory; they hope that a future theory will disclose hidden variables that will allow exact calculations. But most physicists hold that indeterminacy is a property of the atomic world itself. Electrons and subatomic particles apparently do not have a precise location in space and time; they are spread-out waves representing a range of possibilities until they are observed.[20]

Among large groups of atoms in everyday objects, indeterminacy at the atomic level averages out statistically to give predictable large-scale behavior. However, in some biological systems, especially in the genetic and nervous systems, changes in a small number of atoms can have *large-scale effects*. A mutation could arise from a quantum event in which a single molecular bond in a gene is formed or broken, and the effects would be amplified in the phenotype of the growing organism, and might be perpetuated by natural selection. Such evolutionary unpredictability would reflect indeterminacy in nature and not merely the limitation of human knowledge.

In *chaos theory* and *nonlinear thermodynamic systems* far from equilibrium, an infinitesimally small uncertainty concerning initial conditions can have enormous consequences. In chaotic systems, a very small change may be amplified exponentially. This has been called "the butterfly effect" because a butterfly in Brazil might alter the weather a month later in New York. The effect of moving an electron on a distant galaxy might be amplified over a long period of time to alter events on the earth.[21] Deterministic laws can be applied only to closed systems; they are an approximation to reality because actual systems that are extremely sensitive to initial conditions can never be totally isolated from outside influences.

According to Stephen Kellert, the *unpredictability of chaotic systems* is not merely a reflection of temporary human ignorance. Prediction over a long time period would require more information than could be stored on all the electrons of our galaxy, and the calculations would take longer than the phenomena we were trying to predict. Moreover, chaotic systems would amplify the quantum indeterminacies that set limits to the accurate specification of initial conditions in both theory and practice. Kellert also notes that in classical physics the behavior of a larger whole is deduced from predictive causal laws governing interactions of its constituent parts. Chaos theory, by contrast, studies the qualitative form of *large-scale patterns* that may be similar even when the constituents are very different. Chaos theory examines holistic geometrical relationships and systemic properties rather than seeking microreduction to detailed causal mechanisms. Order is a broader concept than law because it includes formal, holistic, historical, and probabilistic patterns.[22]

3. Top-Down Causality

Living organisms exhibit a many-leveled hierarchy of systems and subsystems. A *level* identifies a unit which is relatively integrated, stable, and self-regulating, even though it interacts with other units at the same level and at higher and lower levels. One such hierarchy is identified structurally: particle, atom, molecule, macromolecule, organelle, cell, organ, organism, and ecosystem. Other hierarchies are identified functionally: the reproductive hierarchy (gene, genome, organism, and population), or the neural hierarchy (molecule, synapse, neuron, neural network, and the brain with its changing patterns of interconnections). Human beings also participate in all the social and cultural interactions studied by the social sciences and humanities. A particular discipline or field of inquiry focuses attention on a particular level and its relation to adjacent levels.

We can distinguish three kinds of *reduction between levels.*

Methodological reduction is a research strategy: the study of lower levels in order to better understand relationships at higher levels. Analysis of molecular interactions has been a spectacularly successful strategy in biology, but it is not incompatible with multilevel analysis and the study of larger systems.

Epistemological reduction is a relation between theories: the claim that laws and theories at one level of analysis can be derived from laws and theories at lower levels. I have argued that biological concepts are distinctive and cannot be defined in physical and chemical terms. Distinctive kinds of explanation are valid at differing levels. But interlevel theories may connect adjacent levels, even if they are not derivable from the theories applicable to either level alone. A series of overlapping theories and models unifies the sciences without implying that one level is more fundamental or real than another.[23]

Ontological reduction is a claim about the kinds of reality or the kinds of causality that exist in the world. It is sometimes asserted that an organism is "nothing but organized molecules," or that "only physical forces are causally effective." I have defended ontological pluralism, a multileveled view of reality in which differing (epistemological) levels of analysis are taken to refer to differing (ontological) levels of events and processes in the world, as claimed by critical realism.[24] In evolutionary history, novel forms of order emerged that not only could not have been predicted from laws and theories governing previously existing forms but that also gave rise to genuinely new kinds of behavior and activity in nature. We can acknowledge the distinctive characteristics of living organisms without assuming that life is a separate substance or a "vital force" added to matter, as the vitalists postulated.

Bottom-up causation occurs when many subsystems influence a system. *Top-down causation* is the influence of a system on many subsystems. Higher-level events influence chemical and physical processes at lower levels without violating lower-level laws.[25] Microproperties are not referred to in the specification of the macrostate of the system. Network properties may be realized through a great variety of particular connections. Correlation of behaviors at one level does not require detailed knowledge of all its components. The rules of chess limit the possible moves but leave open an immense number of possibilities that are consistent with but not determined by those rules. So, too, the laws of chemistry limit the combinations of molecules that are found in DNA but do not determine them. The meaning of the message conveyed by DNA is not given by the laws of chemistry but by the operation of the whole system. The communication of signals in neurons requires some expenditure of energy; however, what is communicated is not the energy but the *form* of the signal in relation to input and output processes occurring at higher levels than the signal itself.

The *holistic* and *anti-reductionistic* character of chaos theory has been described by one of its best-known exponents, James Gleick:

> Chaos is anti-reductionist. This new science makes a strong claim about the world; namely, that when it comes to the most interesting questions, questions about order and disorder, decay and creativity, pattern formation and life itself, the whole cannot be explained in terms of the parts. There are fundamental laws about complex systems, but they are new kinds of laws. They are laws of structure and organization and scale, and they simply vanish when you focus on the individual constituents of a complex system—just as the psychology of a lynch mob vanishes when you interview individual participants.[26]

We know little about how memories are preserved in the brain, but computer simulations of neural nets suggest that memory may be stored in *distributed patterns* rather than at discrete locations. In some computer networks with parallel distributed processing, the nodes in a series of layers can be connected by links whose strength can be varied. In one experiment, the inputs are groups of letters, and the outputs are random sounds in a voice synthesizer. Every time the correlation between an input and the correct output is improved, the strongest links are strengthened, so the network gradually improves its performance. The network can be taught to pronounce written words. The connective patterns involve the whole network, and they are learned by experience rather than by being directly programmed. Patterns develop in the whole without prior specification of the parts; the readjustment of the parts can be considered a form of top-down causation.[27] We should also note that the brain of a baby is not finished or "hard-wired" at birth. The neural pathways are developed in interaction with the environment and are altered by the baby's experiences.

Of all the sciences, ecology is the most *holistic* in its outlook. No part of an ecosystem can be considered in isolation because changes in one component often have far-reaching ramifications elsewhere in the system. The participants in an ecosystem are linked by multiple connections and cycles. The oxygen inhaled by animals is exhaled as carbon dioxide, which is in turn taken in by plants and converted back to oxygen. The food chain connects various life-forms. Predator and prey are dependent on each other in maintaining stable populations. A holistic approach is also used in the field of systems analysis which studies the dynamics of urban, industrial, and electronic systems. In all these cases, there are of course lawful relations among the parts, but their behavior is analyzed in relation to a larger whole.

Holism is both a rejection of ontological reductionism and a claim that the whole influences the parts. Attention is directed to the parts of a particular whole, even though it is in turn a part of a larger whole. The whole/part distinction is usually structural and spatial (for example, a *larger* whole). *Top-down causality* is a very similar concept, but it draws attention to a hierarchy of many levels characterized by qualitative differences in organization and activity (for example, a *higher* level). Levels are defined by functional and dynamic relationships. Patterns in time are emphasized, though of course they are inseparable from patterns in space.

Bruce Weber and Terrence Deacon have distinguished three kinds of emergence. In first-order emergence, new properties appear in an aggregate but they can be predicted from lower-level laws and configurational relationships among the components, without knowledge of the previous history of the system. For example, the liquidity of water can be explained by the laws governing hydrogen, oxygen, and their combination into molecules. The thermodynamic laws of gases can be derived from the statistical mechanics of gas molecules. In second-order emergence, system-wide configurations change across time and affect lower-level interactions. Higher-order regularities can become unpredictably unstable and new causal architectures are formed. Chaos theory and complexity theory show critical sensitivity to initial conditions and to historical contingencies. Every falling snowflake is unique because its past history of growth under conditions of variable temperature and humidity constrains its future possibilities.

In *third-order emergence,* according to Weber and Deacon, levels and scales of causality are linked across wider spans of time and space. When features of the state of a system can be represented as a historical memory, the information can be repeatedly re-entered at lower levels of the ongoing system. This occurs in differing ways in biological evolution, in the development of an embryo, and in the cultural transmission of information. In the continuing legacy of interaction between genes, organisms, populations, and environments, causality is distributed across time and space, forming multi-layer systems of great complexity. Adaptation is itself a highly holistic concept, a complex of traits selected in a wider context. Representation, memory, and reference are crucial features of cognitive mental processes expressed in global configurations of neural activity. These authors defend a "progressive holism" of "top-down configurational causes" in addition to bottom-up causes that have a discrete location in time and space.[28]

4. The Communication of Information

Information has been an important term in many fields of science. In the thermodynamics of gases, systems of *low entropy* are highly improbable molecular configurations, which tend to degrade into the more probable configurations of uniform equilibrium states. This entails a loss of order and pattern that is also a loss of information. *Information theory* was first developed in World War II in studies of the communication of messages by radio. Communication is more reliable if the signal-to-noise ratio is high and if a coded message contains regularities and redundancies which allow the detection of errors. With the advent of computers, instructions could be encoded in a binary representation (0/1 or off/on) and quantified as *"bits" of information.* The computer responds to the instructions in the program, which specify the connections in its electrical circuits. It manipulates the electrical representations of the symbols fed into it ("information processing") and then activates some form of output. The letters on a printed page are of course the classical case of the communication of information to a reader.[29]

Information is *an ordered pattern* that is one among many possible sequences or states of a system. The pattern could be a sequence of

DNA bases, alphabetical letters, auditory sounds, binary digits, or any other combinable elements. Information is *communicated* when another system (reader, listener, computer, living cell, etc.) responds selectively—that is, when information is coded, transmitted, and decoded. The meaning of the message is dependent on a wider *context of interpretation*. It must be viewed dynamically and relationally rather than in purely static terms as if the message were contained in the pattern itself.

The information in DNA sequences in genes is significant precisely because of its context in a larger organic system. In the growth of an embryo, a system of time delays, spatial differentiation, and chemical feedback signals communicates the information needed so that the right proteins, cells, and organs are assembled at the right location and time. Complicated developmental pathways, with information flowing in both directions, connect genes with molecular activities and physiological structures. A genome contains an immense number of possible developmental scenarios, of which only a few are realized. In *The Ontogeny of Information*, Susan Oyama argues that the meaning and informational significance of genetic instructions depends on what cells and tissues are already present, and on the actual functioning of the developmental system. In place of a one-way flow of information, we must imagine interactive construction in a particular context.[30]

An enzyme speeds the interaction of two molecules by recognizing them (by shape and chemical affinity) and holding them at adjacent sites where they can react with each other. Molecules of the immune system recognize an invading virus, which is like a key that fits a lock, and they are activated to release a specific antibody. The communication between molecules is dependent on properties of both the sender and the receiver. A receptor is part of an embodied action system that implements a response to signals. In sense perception, transducers in the eye and ear convert physical inputs into neural impulses. In itself the frequency of firing of a neuron tells us very little about the information being communicated. Information is effective only in the context of interpretation and response. Information is constructed from sense data by active and action-oriented processes.[31]

Stored in the DNA is a wealth of *historically acquired information*, including programs for coping with the world. For example, a bird or animal uses specific visual or auditory clues to recognize and respond to a dangerous predator that it has not previously encountered. Individuals in some species are programmed to communicate warning signals to alert other members of the species. Higher primates are capable of symbolic communication of information, and human beings can use words to express abstract concepts. Human information can be transmitted between generations not only by genes and by parental example, but also in speech, literature, art, music, and other cultural forms. The storage and communication of information is thus an important feature of biological processes at many levels and it must always be understood dynamically and relationally rather than in purely static and formal terms. Even at low levels, reality consists not simply of matter and energy, but of matter, energy, and information.

Models of God's Action in Nature

What models of God's relation to nature are compatible with the central affirmations of the Christian tradition and also with a world which is characterized by self-organization, indeterminacy, top-down causality, and communication of information? I will examine theological proposals that draw from each of these four characteristics.

All four models reject the idea of *divine intervention* that violates the laws of nature. In none of them is God invoked to fill particular gaps in the scientific account (the "God of the gaps" who is vulnerable to the advance of science). God's role is different from that of natural causes. In each case, a feature of current scientific theory is taken as a model (that is, a systematically developed analogy) of God's action in nature.[32] Some authors in the first group below do propose a new version of *natural theology* in which evidence from science is used as an argument in support of theism, even if it does not offer a proof of God's existence. The other authors are proposing ways in which a God who is accepted on other grounds (such as religious experience in a historical interpretive community) might be reconceived as acting in nature. I have called such an approach *a theology of nature* rather than a natural theology.[33]

1. God as Designer of a Self-Organizing Process

Until the nineteenth century, the intricate organization and effective functioning of living creatures were taken as evidence of an intelligent designer. After Darwin, the argument was reformulated: God did not create things in their present forms but designed an evolutionary process through which all living forms came into being. Today we know that life is possible only under a very narrow range of physical and chemical conditions. We have seen also that in the self-organization of molecules leading to life there seems to have been considerable built-in design in biochemical affinities, molecular structures, and potential for complexity and hierarchical order. The world of molecules seems to have an inherent tendency to move toward emergent complexity, life, and consciousness.

If design is understood as a detailed pre-existing plan in the mind of God, *chance* is the antithesis of *design*. But if design is identified with the general direction of growth toward complexity, life, and consciousness, then both law and chance can be part of design. Disorder is sometimes a condition for the emergence of new forms of order, as in thermodynamic systems far from equilibrium, or in the mutations of evolutionary history. We can no longer accept the clockmaker God who designed every detail of a determinate mechanism. But one option today is a revised deism in which God designed the world as *a many-leveled creative process of law and chance*. Paul Davies is an exponent of this position.[34]

A patient God could endow matter with diverse potentialities and let the world create itself. We can say that God respects the integrity of the world and allows it to be itself, without interfering with it, just as God respects human freedom and allows us to be ourselves. Moral responsibility requires that the world have some openness, which takes the form of chance at lower levels and choice at the human level. But responsible choice also requires enough lawfulness that we have some idea of the probable consequences of our decisions.

An attractive feature of this option is that it provides at least partial answers to the problems of *suffering and death*, which were such a challenge to the classical argument from design. For competition and death are intrinsic to an evolutionary process. Pain is an inescapable concomitant of greater sensitivity and awareness, and it provides a valuable warning of external dangers. My main objection to a reformulated deism is that we are left with a distant and inactive God, a far cry from the active God of the Bible who continues to be intimately involved with the world and human life.

One could still argue that God has an ongoing role in *sustaining* the world and its laws. Some theologians maintain that the world does not stand on its own but needs God's continual concurrence to maintain and uphold it in what is known today to be a dynamic rather than a static process. Others defend Thomas Aquinas's belief that God as *primary cause* works through the matrix of *secondary causes* in the natural world. According to neo-Thomists such as William Stoeger, there are no gaps in the scientific account on its own level; God's action is on a totally different plane from all secondary causes.[35] Many neo-Thomists maintain that divine sovereignty is maintained if all events are foreseen and predetermined in God's plan. God does not have to intervene or interfere with the laws of nature; divine action occurs indirectly and instrumentally through natural processes. This view respects the integrity of science and the transcendence of God, whose action is not like causality within the world. Some theologians hold that God sees all events in timeless eternity without determining them, but I would argue that predestination is not compatible with human freedom or the presence of chance, evil, and suffering in the world.

2. God as Determiner of Indeterminacies

I suggested earlier that uncertainties in the predictions made by quantum theory reflect indeterminacy in nature itself, rather than the inadequacy of current theory. In that interpretation, *a range of possibilities* is present in the world. Quantum events have necessary but not sufficient physical causes. If they are not completely determined by the relationships described by the laws of physics, their final determination might be made directly by God. What appears to be chance, which atheists take as an argument against theism, may be the very point at which God acts.

Divine sovereignty would be maintained if God *providentially controls* the events that appear to us as chance. No energy input would be needed, since the alternative potentialities in a quantum state have identical energy. God does not have to intervene as a physical force pushing electrons around but instead actualizes one of the many potentialities already present—determining, for example, the instant at which a particular radioactive atom decays.[36]

We have seen that under some conditions the effects of very small differences at the microlevel are greatly amplified in *large-scale phenomena.* In nonlinear thermodynamics and chaos theory, an infinitesimal initial change can produce dramatic changes in the larger system. Similar trigger effects occur in evolutionary mutations and in genetic and neural systems today. Scientific research finds only law and chance, but perhaps in God's knowledge all events are foreseen and predetermined through a combination of law and particular divine action. Since God's action would be scientifically undetectable, it could be neither proved nor refuted by science. This would exclude any proof of God's action of the kind sought in natural theology, but it would not exclude the possibility of God's action affirmed on other grounds in a wider theology of nature.

If we assume that *God controls all indeterminacies,* we could preserve the traditional idea of predestination. This would be theological determinism rather than physical determinism, since nothing happens by chance. But then the problems of waste, suffering, and human freedom would remain acute. Nancey Murphy has proposed that God determines all quantum indeterminacies but arranges that lawlike regularities usually result, in order to make stable structures and scientific investigation possible and to ensure that human actions have dependable consequences so that moral choices are possible. Orderly relationships do not constrain God, since they are included in God's purposes. God grants causal powers to created entities. Murphy holds that in human life God acts both at the quantum level and at higher levels of mental activity but does so in such a way that human freedom is not violated.[37]

An alternative would be to say that most quantum events occur by chance, but *God influences some of them* without violating the statistical laws of quantum physics. This view has been defended by Robert Russell, George Ellis, and Thomas Tracy, and it is consistent with the scientific evidence.[38] A possible objection to this model is that it assumes *bottom-up causality* within nature once God's action has occurred and thus seems to concede the reductionist's claim that the behavior of all entities is determined by their smallest parts (or lowest levels). The action would be bottom-up even if one assumed that God's intentions were directed to the larger wholes (or higher levels) affected by these quantum events. Most of these authors also allow for God's action at higher levels, however, which then results in a *top-down influence* on lower levels, in addition to quantum effects from the bottom up. The model can thus be combined with one of the models discussed below.

3. God as Top-Down Cause

The idea of levels of reality can be extended if God is viewed as acting from an even higher level than nature. Arthur Peacocke holds that God exerts a *top-down causality* on the world. God's action would be a constraint on relationships at lower levels that does not violate lower-level laws. Constraints may be introduced not just at spatial or temporal boundaries but also internally through any additional specification allowed by lower-level laws. In human beings, God would influence their highest evolutionary level, that of mental activity, which would affect the neural networks and neurons in the brain.[39] Within human beings, divine action would be effected down the hierarchy of natural levels, concerning which we have at least some understanding of relationships between adjacent levels. (Peacocke gives a table showing the hierarchy of academic disciplines, from the physical sciences to the humanities, which study successively higher levels, with some disciplines addressing inter-level questions.[40]) His use of top-down causality seems to me more problematic in the case of divine action on inanimate matter; we would have to assume direct influence between the highest level (God) and the lowest level (matter) in the absence of intermediate levels—which has no analogy within the natural order.

Peacocke also extends to God the idea of *whole-part* relationships found in nature. He proposes that God as "the most inclusive whole" acts on "the-world-as-a-whole." But this spatial analogy seems dubious because the world does not have spatial boundaries, and it has no temporal ones if we accept Stephen Hawking's version of quantum cosmology. Moreover, the rejection of universal simultaneity in relativity theory makes it impossible to speak of "the-world-as-a-whole" at any one moment. The whole is a spatiotemporal continuum with temporal as well as spatial dimensions. In such a framework God's action would presumably have to be more localized in space and time, interacting more directly with a particular part rather than indirectly through action on the spatiotemporal whole.

One version of top-down causality uses the relation of mind to body in human beings as an analogy for God's relation to the world. Some authors urge us to look on *the world as God's body*, and God as the world's mind or soul. In using the analogy, we can make allowance for the human limitations that would not apply to God. We have direct awareness of our thoughts and feelings but only limited awareness of many other events in our bodies, whereas God would be directly aware of all events. We did not choose our bodies and we can affect only a limited range of events in them, whereas God's actions are said to affect all events universally. From the pattern of behavior of other people we infer their intentions, which cannot be directly observed; similarly, the cosmic drama can be interpreted as the expression of God's intentions.[41]

But the analogy breaks down if it is pressed too far. The cosmos as a whole lacks the intermediate levels of organization found in the body. It does not have the biochemical or neurological channels of feedback and communication through which the activities of organisms are coordinated and integrated. To be sure, an omnipresent God would not need the cosmic equivalent of a nervous system. God is presumably not as dependent on particular bodily structures as we are. However, we would be abandoning the analogy if we said that God is a disembodied mind acting directly on the separate physical components of the world. It appears that we need a more pluralistic analogy allowing for interaction among a community of beings, rather than a monistic analogy that pictures us all as parts of one being. The world and God seem more like a community with a dominant member than like a single organism.

4. God as Communicator of Information

In radio transmissions, computers, and biological systems, the *communication of information* between two points requires a physical input and an expenditure of energy (the so-called Brillouin-Szilard relationship). But if God is omnipresent (including presence everywhere at the microlevel), no energy would be required for the communication of information. Moreover, the realization of alternative potentialities already present in the quantum world would convey differing information without any physical input or expenditure of energy.

Arthur Peacocke has used a rich variety of analogies in addition to top-down causality. Some of these involve the communication of information. God is like the choreographer of a dance in which much of the action is left up to the dancers, or the composer of a still-unfinished symphony, experimenting, improvising, and expanding on a theme and variations.[42] Peacocke suggests that the purposes of God are *communicated through the pattern of events* in the world. We can look on evolutionary history as the action of an agent who expresses intentions but does not follow an exact predetermined plan. Moreover, an input of information from God could influence the relationships among our memories, images, and concepts, just as our thoughts influence the activity of neurons. Peacocke maintains that Jesus Christ was a powerfully God-informed person who was a uniquely effective vehicle for God's self-expression, so that in Christ God's purposes are more clearly revealed than in nature or elsewhere in history.[43]

John Polkinghorne proposes that God's action is *an input of "pure information."* We have seen that in chaos theory an infinitesimally small energy input produces a very large change in the system. Polkinghorne suggests that in imagining God's action we might extrapolate chaos theory to the limiting case of zero energy. (This differs from quantum theory, in which there actually is *zero* energy difference between alternative potentialities, so no extrapolation is needed). Polkinghorne holds that God's action is a nonenergetic input of information that expresses holistic patterns. God's selection among the envelope of possibilities present in chaotic processes could bring about novel structures and types of order exemplifying systemic higher-level organizing principles.[44]

The biblical idea of divine Word or *Logos* resembles the concept of information. In Greek thought, the *Logos* was a universal rational principle, but biblical usage also expressed the Hebrew understanding of Word as creative power. The Word in both creation and redemption can indeed be thought of as the communication of information from God to the world. As in the case of genetic information and human language, the meaning of the message must be discerned within a wider context of interpretation. God's Word to human beings preserves their freedom because it evokes but does not compel their response.[45] But the divine *Logos* is not simply the communication of an impersonal message since it is inseparable from an ongoing personal relationship. The *Logos* is not a structure of abstract ideas like Plato's eternal forms, or like a computer program that exists independently of its embodiment in a particular medium or hardware system. If we believe that one of God's purposes was to create loving and responsible persons, not simply intelligent information processors, we will have to draw our analogies concerning the communication of information primarily from human life, rather than from the genetic code or computer programs.

God's Action in Process Theology

Process theology is the attempt of theologians to use the process philosophy of Alfred North Whitehead in the expression and reformulation of a religious tradition—particularly the Christian tradition, though some Jewish and Buddhist thinkers have also been interested in process philosophy. Process theology shows some similarities with each of the four themes above, but it differs because it adds a fifth idea, that of interiority.

1. Biology and Process Philosophy

Many features of contemporary science are strongly represented in process philosophy. Whitehead was indebted to quantum physics for his portrayal of the discrete, episodic, and indeterminate character of all events. He was indebted to relativity for his view that all entities are constituted by their relationships. Process thought is evolutionary in stressing temporality and change. Becoming and activity are considered more fundamental than being and substance. The continuity of evolutionary history implies the impossibility of drawing absolute lines between successive life-forms historically, or between levels of reality today.[46] Each of the four themes outlined earlier can be found in process philosophy:

Self-organization is a characteristic of the basic units of reality, which are momentarily unified events (Whitehead called them "actual occasions," but I will refer to them simply as "events," which reminds us of their temporal character). No event is merely a passive product of its past. All events are also products of present creative activity in which organization is realized—that is, pattern and structure that are temporal as well as spatial. But self-organization is analyzed by process thought in a distinctive way. Interiority is postulated in every event, providing a unifying center for the organizing activity.

Indeterminacy is assumed by process thought not only in the quantum world but at all levels of integrated activity. Both order and openness are present at all levels. At lower levels, order predominates, while at higher levels there is more opportunity for spontaneity, creativity, and novelty.

Top-down causality is defended in process writings. Process thought is *holistic* in portraying a network of interconnected events. Every event is a new synthesis of the influences on it; it occurs in a context which affects it and which it in turn affects. This can be called a relational or ecological view of reality. Not even God is self-contained, for God's experience is affected by the world. More specifically, reality is taken to be *multileveled*. Events at high levels of complexity are dependent on events at lower levels. But genuinely new phenomena emerge at higher levels that cannot be explained by the laws describing lower-level phenomena. Charles Hartshorne's version of process philosophy makes extensive use of the concept of hierarchical levels with differing characteristics, and he gives a careful critique of reductionism.[47]

The communication of information is not prominent in early process writings, which is not surprising since its scientific importance was not recognized prior to World War II. However, the idea that a concrescing event takes other events into account resembles the contextual and relational character of information in action. James Hutchingson notes that information always involves selection from among possible states; he proposes that Whitehead's "actual occasions" are information-processing entities that select from among the possibilities provided by God and previous events. Moreover, information from the world feeds back to God; this feedback leads to relevant readjustment, as in cybernetic systems. Hutchingson finds holism and top-down causality in the role of information in both process thought and systems theory. A system works as a whole to restrict the ability of its components to realize all possible states. New forms of order are generated at higher levels of organization, according to both process and systems thinking.[48]

2. Interiority

Interiority is the most controversial theme in process thought. Reality is construed as a network of interconnected events that are also *moments of experience,* each integrating in its own way the influences from its past and from other entities. The evolution of interiority, like the evolution of physical structures, is said to be characterized by both continuity and change. The forms taken by interiority vary widely, from rudimentary memory, sentience, responsiveness, and anticipation in simpler organisms, to consciousness and self-consciousness in more complex ones. Human life is the only point at which we know reality from within. If we start from the presence of both physical structures and experience in human life, we can imagine simpler and simpler structures in which experience is more and more rudimentary. But if we start with simple physical structures totally devoid of interiority, it is difficult to see how the complexification of external structures can result in interiority.[49]

The approach and avoidance reactions of bacteria can be considered elementary forms of perception and response. An amoeba learns to find sugar, indicating a rudimentary memory and intentionality. Invertebrates seem to have some sentience and capacity for pain and pleasure. Purposiveness and anticipation are clearly present among lower vertebrates, and the presence of a nervous system greatly enhances these capacities. The behavior of animals gives evidence that they suffer intensely, and even invertebrates under stress release endorphins and other pain-suppressant chemicals similar to those in human brains. Some species exhibit considerable problem-solving and anticipatory abilities and a range of awareness and feelings. Conceptualizing interiority requires that we try to look on an organism's activities from its own point of view, even though its experience must be very different from our own.[50]

We noted earlier that evolutionary change can be *initiated by the activity of organisms* in selecting their own environments (the Baldwin effect). Their diverse responses and novel actions may create new evolutionary possibilities. Among the creatures who were the common ancestors of bison and horses, some charged their enemies head on, and their survival would have been enhanced by strength, weight, strong skulls, and other bison-like qualities. Others in the same population fled from their enemies, and their survival depended on speed, agility, and other abilities we see in horses. The divergence of bison and horse may have arisen initially from different responses to danger, rather than from genetic mutations related to anatomy. Emotions and mental responses are not uniquely determined by the genes, though they occur in nervous systems that are the product of an inherited set of genes. Organisms participate actively in evolutionary history and are not simply passive products of genetic forces from within and environmental forces from without.[51]

We are each aware of our experience despite the difficulty of studying it scientifically. It is this direct awareness that leads us to attribute subjectivity to other humans, animals, and even to lower forms of life. While the terms *consciousness* and *mind* should be restricted to organisms with a nervous system, it is reasonable to attribute rudimentary forms of perception and experience to organisms as simple as the amoeba. I would argue that in the light of evolutionary continuity and in the interest of metaphysical generality we should take *experience* as a category applicable to all integrated entities, even if consciousness appears only in higher life-forms.

3. Christianity and Process Theology

Some features of God's relation to the world in process thought seem to represent the operation of an impersonal principle. God is the source of order and also the source of novelty in the world. God presents new possibilities but leaves alternatives open, eliciting the response of entities in the world. But the God of process thought is actually very personal and responsive to ongoing events in the world. God is present in the unfolding of every event but never exclusively determines the outcome. This is a God of persuasion rather than coercion. For process theologians, God is not as an omnipotent ruler but the leader and inspirer of an interdependent community of beings. John Cobb and David Griffin speak of God as "creative-responsive love," which affects the world but is also affected by it. God's relation to human beings is used as a model for God's relation to all beings.[52]

Process theologians stress God's *immanence* and participation in the world, but they do not give up *transcendence*. God is said to be temporal in being affected by interaction with the world but eternal and unchanging in character and purpose. Classical ideas of omnipresence and omniscience are retained, but not even God can know a future which is still open. Compared to the traditional Western model, God's power over events in the world is severely limited, especially at lower levels where events are almost exclusively determined by their past. The long span of cosmic history suggests a patient and subtle God working through the slow emergence of novel forms. Christian process theologians hold that the life and death of Christ are the supreme examples of the power of God's love and participation in the life of the world. The cross is a revelation of suffering love, and the resurrection reveals that even death does not end that love.

Process thought shares insights with each of the theological models described earlier, but it differs at crucial points.

Like God *the designer of a self-organizing process,* the God of process thought is the source of order in the world. But the process God is also directly involved in the emergence of novelty through the interiority of each unified event. Deism is avoided because God has a direct and continuing role in the history of the world.

Like those who say that God *determines quantum indeterminacies,* process thinkers hold that God influences systems that are not fully determined by past events. It is never an absolute determination, for God always works along with other causes. In process thought God's activity occurs at higher levels of organization in addition to the quantum level. This avoids a reliance on quantum events alone, which would perpetuate the reductionist's assumption that only bottom-up causality operates within natural systems.

Like those who postulate God as *top-down cause,* process thinkers stress God's immanence and participation in an interdependent many-leveled world. But process thought has no difficulty conceptualizing the interaction between the highest level (God) and the lowest (inanimate matter) in the absence of intermediate levels, because God is present in the unfolding of integrated events at all levels. Hartshorne has indeed used the analogy of *the world as God's body,* though we must remember that in the process scheme the body is itself a community of integrated entities at various levels. Most process theologians, however, insist on a greater divine transcendence and greater human freedom than the analogy of a cosmic body suggests. Using a social rather than organic analogy they imagine us, not as cells in God's body, but as members of a cosmic community of which God is the pre-eminent member.

The idea that God *communicates information* to the world is consistent with process thought. God's ordering and valuation of potentialities is a form of information within a larger context of meaning. God also receives information from the world, and God is changed by such feedback. The communication of information occurs within the momentary experience of integrated events at any level rather than by bottom-up causality through quantum phenomena alone or through the trigger points of chaos theory or by top-down causality acting on the whole cosmos. God, past events, and the event's present response join in the formation of every event. Process thought uses a single conceptual representation for divine action at all levels, whereas some of the authors mentioned earlier assume very different modes of divine action at various levels in the world. At the same time, process thought tries to allow for differences in the character of events that occur at diverse levels.

The role of God in process thought has much in common with the biblical understanding of *the Holy Spirit*. Like the process God, the Spirit works from within. In various biblical passages, the Spirit is said to indwell, renew, empower, inspire, guide, and reconcile. According to Psalm 104, the Spirit creates in the present: "Thou dost cause the grass to grow for the cattle, and plants for man to cultivate . . . . When thou sendest forth thy Spirit, they are created; and thou renewest the face of the ground." The Spirit represents God's presence and activity in the world. This is an emphasis on immanence which, like that in process theology, does not rule out transcendence. Moreover, the Spirit is God at work in nature, in human experience, and in Christ, so creation and redemption are aspects of a single activity.[53] Process thought similarly applies a single set of concepts to God's role in human and nonhuman life, and it is not incompatible with the idea of particular divine action and human response in the life of Christ. The Holy Spirit comes to us from without to evoke our response from within. It is symbolized by the dove, the gentlest of birds. Other symbols of the Spirit are wind and fire, which can be more overpowering, but they usually represent inspiration rather than sheer power. I have elsewhere tried to show that the process view of God is consistent with other aspects of the biblical message.[54]

4. Some Objections

Let me finally note some possible objections to process thought.

1. Is panexperientialism credible? Process thinkers attribute rudimentary experience, feeling, and responsiveness to simple entities. They hold that mind and consciousness are present only at higher levels in more complex organisms, so they are not panpsychists (who ascribe at least rudimentary forms of mind at even the lowest level). Rocks and inanimate objects are mere aggregates with no unified experience. There are no sharp lines between forms of life in evolutionary history or among creatures today. It appears that for matter to produce mind, in evolution or in embryological development, there must be intermediate stages or levels, and mind and matter must have some characteristics in common. No extrapolation of physical concepts can yield the concepts needed to describe our subjective experience. Process thought interprets lower-level events as simpler cases of higher-level ones, rather than trying to interpret higher-level events in terms of lower-level concepts or resorting to dualism.

Yet Whitehead himself was so intent on elaborating a set of metaphysical categories applicable to all events that I believe he gave insufficient attention to the radically different ways in which those categories are exemplified at different levels. In that regard, Hartshorne, Griffin, and other more recent process thinkers are more helpful. I have also questioned whether Whitehead's understanding of the episodic character of moments of experience provides an adequate view of human selfhood. I would argue that we can accept more continuity and a stronger route of inheritance of personal identity, without reverting to traditional categories of substance (see chapter 4 below).

2. *Is this a God of the gaps?* In earlier centuries, God was invoked as an explanation for what was scientifically unexplained. It was held that God intervened at discrete points in an otherwise law-abiding sequence. This was a losing strategy when the gaps in the scientific account were successively closed. According to process philosophy, by contrast, God does not intervene unilaterally to fill particular gaps. God is already present in the unfolding of every event, but no event is attributable to God alone. God and the creatures are co-creators. The role filled by God is not a gap of the kind that might be filled by science, which studies the causal influence of the past. The contribution of God cannot be separated out as if it were another external force, for it operates through the interiority of every entity, which is not accessible to science. God's influence on lower-level events would be minimal, so it is not surprising that the evolution of new forms has been such a long, slow process.

3. *Can we worship a God of limited power?* The God envisaged by process thought is less powerful than the omnipotent ruler of classical theology. But different kinds of power are effective in different ways. The power revealed in Christ is the power of love to evoke our response, rather than the power to control us externally. Moreover, the God of process thought is everlasting, omnipresent, unchanging in purpose, knows all that can be known, and has a universal role and priority in status reminiscent of many of the traditional divine attributes. But I would grant that the numinous experience of the holy and the Christian experience of worship seem to require a greater emphasis on transcendence than we find in Whitehead himself. We can adapt Whiteheadian categories to the theological task of interpreting the experience of the Christian community without accepting all of his ideas. The question of God's power is explored further in chapter 5.

4. *Is process thought too philosophical?* Metaphysical categories seem abstract and theoretical, far removed from the existential issues of personal life that are central in religion. Some process writers use a technical vocabulary that is understandable only after considerable study, though process ideas can be expressed in a more familiar vocabulary. No theologian can avoid the use of philosophical categories in the systematic elaboration of ideas. Augustine drew from Plato, Aquinas from Aristotle, Barth from Kant, and so forth. But we do always need to return to the starting point of theological reflection in the formative events and characteristic experiences of the Christian community. Imaginative models are more important than abstract concepts in the daily life of the church. No model is a literal or exhaustive representation, and we can use different models to imagine different aspects of God's relation to the world. In our search for universality we must be in dialogue with people in other social locations, since economic interests, cultural values, and gender affect all our interpretive categories.

We have examined a variety of models of God's action in an evolutionary world, with particular attention to the process view. Perhaps, after all, we should return to the biblical concept of the Holy Spirit. This will help us to avoid the separation of creation and redemption that occurred in much of classical Christianity. It will help us recover a sense of the sacred in nature that can motivate a strong concern for the environment today. The Spirit is God working from within in both human life and the natural world, which is consistent with process thought. The theme of the 1991 assembly of the World Council of Churches in Canberra, Australia, was a prayer in which we can join: "Come, Holy Spirit, renew thy whole creation."

3

Evolution, Genetics, and Human Nature

Evolution has not only challenged classical concepts of God. It has also called into question traditional teachings about human nature. This chapter considers the theological implications of research on human evolution and the influence of genes on human behavior. Are we determined by our genes, inherited from more primitive ancestors? How should we view the new powers that knowledge of genetics is giving us, such as the possibility of modifying human genes or cloning human beings?

Human Evolution

In Darwin's day, evolution presented a challenge to the traditional understanding of the status of humanity. Since then, evidence for human descent from prehuman ancestors has accumulated from many scientific disciplines. From molecular biology we know that chimpanzees and humans today share more than 99 percent of their DNA, though of course the 1 percent that differs is critical. Anthropologists in Africa have found a variety of fossil forms intermediate between chimpanzees and humans. *Australopithecus afarensis,* an ape-like creature, was walking on two legs some four million years ago. In Ethiopia, bones were found from a short female, dubbed Lucy, who walked on two legs, had long arms and a brain size like that of the great apes, while her teeth show that she was a meat eater. It appears that the move from trees to grassland led to upright posture, which allowed greater freedom to manipulate objects, greater reliance on vision, and a shift to hunting, long before the development of a larger brain. *Homo erectus,* two million years ago, had a much larger brain, lived in long-term group sites, made more complicated tools, and probably used fire.

Archaic forms of *Homo sapiens* appeared 400,000 years ago, and the Neanderthals were in Europe 150,000 years ago (though they were probably not in the line of descent to modern humans). The Cromagnons made paintings on cave walls and performed burial rituals 30,000 years ago. The earliest known writing, Sumerian, is 6,000 years old. Techniques for melting metallic ores brought the Bronze Age and then, less than 3,000 years ago, the Iron Age. Here we have at least the broad outlines of the evolution of both physiology and behavior from nonhuman to human forms and the beginnings of human culture.[1]

Apart from such discoveries of fossils and artifacts, research on human origins has been carried out in four fields discussed below: sociobiology, primate studies, anthropological studies of language and culture, and studies of the evolution of religion.

1. Sociobiology and Human Morality

If evolution is the survival of the fittest, how can we explain *altruistic behavior* in which an organism jeopardizes its own survival? Social insects, such as ants, will sacrifice themselves to protect the colony. Edward O. Wilson and others have shown that such behavior reduces the number of descendants an individual will have, but it enhances the survival of close relatives who carry many of the same genes. If I share half of my genes with my brother or sister, it will perpetuate my genes if I am willing to protect their reproductive futures, even at some risk to my own life. If I help people to whom I am not related, they will in the future be more likely to help me (reciprocal altruism), but this too will contribute indirectly to the survival of my genes.[2]

Wilson is confident that evolutionary biology will account for all aspects of human life. Both religion and ethics will be explained and eventually replaced by biological knowledge. In the past, he says, morality has been an expression of emotions encoded in the genes. "The only demonstrated function of morality is to keep the genes intact." But now science can "search for the bedrock of ethics—by which I mean the material basis of natural law."[3] Richard Dawkins entitled one of his books *The Selfish Gene* because he believes that all apparently altruistic behavior can be explained by its contribution to genetic survival.[4]

Authors in the new field of *evolutionary psychology* share many of the assumptions of sociobiology, but they assign a greater role to culture in determining the specific ways in which our genetic heritage affects our behavior. A cover story by Robert Wright appeared in *Time* magazine with the title "Infidelity: It May Be in Our Genes." Wright claims that adultery is natural because behavior favoring a higher number of genetic descendants was selected in Stone Age society. He says that men are particularly prone to promiscuity because they can proliferate their genes with a relatively small investment in the birth and care of children. Women are more likely to seek men with power and status, who can be good providers for their children. Wright also claims that there is a genetic basis for criminality, but he holds that belief in free will is a useful fiction because it allows us to assign responsibility and punishment, which are deterrents to criminal behavior.[5]

The evolutionary philosopher Michael Ruse argues that all values are *subjective*, but the fact that we think they are *objective* can be explained by sociobiology. Values are actually human constructions that we project on the world, he says, but in order to take them seriously we have to believe that they are objective. Evolutionary selection has favored the cultural myth of objective values. "Darwinian theory shows that in fact morality is a function of (subjective) feelings, but it shows also that we have (and must have) the illusion of objectivity. . . . In a sense, therefore, morality is a collective illusion foisted upon us by our genes."[6] Ruse says that the belief that God is the source of moral rules makes such rules more socially effective and thus serves a useful biological function. It would seem, however, that Ruse's position is self-defeating, for once the secret is out that ethical norms are a collective illusion, we can hardly expect their social effectiveness to continue.

In replying to the sociobiologists, Elliott Sober and David Wilson argue that selection occurs *at many levels* in addition to the genes that enhance the survival of genetic relatives. Cooperation occurs among members of a group that are not all genetically related—for example, in cooperative hunting and meat-sharing in hunter-gatherer societies—and social rules provide restraints on individualism. These authors insist that we must make a clear distinction between biological consequences for survival and psychological motives for actions. In contrast to the attempt of sociobiologists to find in apparently altruistic human actions some covert selfish motive (such as earning the esteem of others or an eternal reward), Sober and Wilson conclude that at the psychological level motives are diverse and include both self-interest (egoism) and altruism (care for the well-being of another as an end in itself).[7]

Holmes Rolston holds that terms such as *selfish genes* or *altruism* are misleading metaphors when applied to lower organic forms because at those levels there are no moral agents with the capacity for choice.

He claims that the capacity for morality, but not particular moral judgments, is the product of natural selection—just as there is a genetic basis for the capacity for language but not for particular languages, and a genetic basis for the capacity to reason but not for particular rational arguments. He finds implausible the claims that all human altruism is really covert self-interest or the expectation of future reciprocation or social approval. Such explanations simply do not fit the Good Samaritan in the biblical story or the life of Mother Theresa or the person who saves the life of a drowning stranger.

Rolston maintains that *cultural evolution* differs significantly from biological evolution. First, cultural innovation replaces mutations and genetic recombination as the source of variability. Such innovations are to some extent deliberate and directional; they are certainly not random. New ideas, institutions, and forms of behavior are often creative and imaginative responses to social problems and crises. Next, in the competition between ideas, selection occurs through social experience. The most useful ideas are retained in a trial-and-error process, but many factors enter into social judgments of success. Here selection is less harsh than biological selection because ideas can be rejected without the death of the individuals who hold them.[8]

Finally, according to Rolston, transmission of *cultural information* occurs through language, tradition, education, and social institutions rather than through genes. Change is more rapid, deliberate, and cumulative than in the case of biological evolution. Major changes can take place within a few generations or even within a generation. On the other hand, old ideas can surface again and be revived, so they are not permanently lost, as are the genes of extinct species. Because of these differences, cultural beliefs can override or offset the genetic tendencies inherited from our prehuman and Stone Age ancestors.

2. Apes and Humans

Research on apes both in the wild and in captivity has shown that they have remarkable capacities, many of which are similar to those of human beings. Such findings support the thesis that humans have evolved from ape-like ancestors. Do they also undermine claims for human uniqueness?

Jane Goodall studied the *social life of chimpanzees* in the forests of Tanzania. She found that they kiss, embrace, and hold hands in contexts that suggest expressions of affection. They laugh, tickle, and play tricks on each other. They seem to experience what we know in humans as emotions of happiness, sadness, anger, and fear. They are responsive to the facial expressions and emotions of others, for example, patting and comforting an individual in distress. They form family bonds, social hierarchies, and strategic coalitions. They are adept in nonverbal communication by gestures and postures and they can use objects as simple tools. Goodall found a darker side of chimp behavior in sexual violence, territorial aggression, and the killing of chimps in other groups. But she also found examples of compassion and empathy, including cases in which an orphaned infant was adopted by a male from another group. She observed the rapt attention and the ecstatic dance of chimps at the foot of a thundering waterfall and postulated a sense of awe and wonder.[9]

Franz de Waal studies chimps in captivity and finds in their behavior *the forerunners of human morality.* Whereas sociobiologists have claimed that we have inherited from prehuman ancestors an inherently selfish nature that can only be partially overcome by culture, de Waal finds in chimps capacities for compassion and kindness from which human morality could have developed. He gives examples of sympathy and care that go far beyond sharing food or cooperating for social goals. A monkey in Japan with deformed hands and legs was adopted by another tribe. A gorilla in a zoo returned an injured human child to her mother. Chimps attempt to mediate or intervene in fights between combative males and they promote reconciliation afterward. They develop codes of social interaction, and they discipline those who violate the rules—whose subsequent behavior looks very much like guilt or shame. De Waal acknowledges that sympathy seldom goes beyond the primate group, but he says it does point to positive social attitudes that in human culture can be extended in a wider circle of concern.[10]

Chimps have been taught to use *sign language,* but there is an ongoing debate as to whether this can be considered an elementary linguistic capacity. The larynx of apes does not allow the modulation of sounds required for the oral communication of words, though like many other species they have distinctive cries or gestures to signal particular dangers or needs. R. A. and P. T. Gardner taught a chimp thirty-four manual signs, which it could combine in twos or threes; but it never acquired syntax (in which the order of the sequence is critical to its meaning).[11] E. Sue Savage-Rumbaugh laboriously taught Kanzi 200 visual symbols, which could be selected in two-symbol combinations (whereas a human two-year old learns rapidly and soon moves on to longer sequences). Most of Kanzi's combinations were requests for immediately accessible objects or actions, though chimps do have some capacity for understanding abstract relationships between the referents of the signs.[12] In short, chimps have remarkable communicative abilities, but they fall far short of human symbolic language. Moreover, the signs used in these experiments were supplied by their human trainers. Language is an inherently social phenomenon and the cultural patterns of our ancestors must have evolved along with the organization of their brains and the creation of language systems without an instructor.

Chimps seem to have a rudimentary *self-awareness*. If a chimp sees in a mirror a mark previously placed on its forehead, it will try to remove the mark. But in human beings self-consciousness goes much further than this. The greater capacity to remember the past, to anticipate the future, and to use abstract symbols liberates us from our immediate time and place. We can imagine possibilities only distantly related to present experience, and we can reflect on goals going far beyond immediate needs. Humans are aware of their finitude and the inevitability of death, and they ask questions about the meaning of their lives. They construct symbolic worlds through language and the arts.

3. Language and Culture

The anthropologist Terrence Deacon sees *symbolic representation* as the crucial factor in the three-way interaction of language, brain physiology, and culture in evolutionary history. Unlike icons and indices, which remain closely associated with objects and events in the world, symbols provide a more abstract level of representation. Symbols can be related to each other in novel ways with only indirect reference to the world. Symbols allow us to consider a wide range of alternative actions and try them out mentally before acting. We can imagine alternative futures and possible worlds. Because symbols can be combined and manipulated with such rich diversity, they are essential for true linguistic communication.

Deacon holds that *brain physiology* was itself influenced by language use. He rejects the thesis that language was simply a by-product of larger brains that evolved for other purposes. The human brain is not just larger; it is organized in a new way—for example, it has a great variety of connections between the prefrontal cortex and other parts of the brain. "The remarkable expansion of the brain that took place in human evolution and indirectly produced prefrontal expansion was not the cause of symbolic language but a consequence of it."[13] Symbolization also enriched the realm of consciousness, which was no longer episodic or focused primarily on local events. A new level of self-determination was possible as alternative futures could be compared and a more explicit self-representation was achieved.

Deacon also insists that symbolic language is intrinsically *social*. It facilitated the communication that enhanced social cooperation in hunting, tool-making, and early human settlements. But it also provided a new channel for transmitting information between generations in addition to genetic inheritance. With symbolic transmission the burden of adaptive change shifted from genes to culture, in which changes could occur much more rapidly. Rituals and narrative stories as well as parental instruction conveyed cultural patterns between generations.

Merlin Donald postulates two types of prehuman culture. The *episodic culture* of apes was event-oriented and action-based. Episodic memory is short-term and situation-bound. Limited communication occurs by signs representing specific events. Cooperative social behavior is directed to immediate needs. The *mimetic culture* of *Homo erectus* two million years ago included more complex forms of non-verbal representation and communication. Here, Donald suggests, relationships were re-enacted in gesture, mime, and dance. Role-playing and the modeling of social status might have resembled the games of prelinguistic children today. Rituals united groups in the public expression of communal responses.

Donald sees a dramatic change in the emergence of *mythic culture* in Cromagnon life 30,000 years ago. The invention of symbols provided the capacity for more abstract thought and wider semantic networks of reference. Spoken language co-evolved with effective vocal apparatus and the development of the brain structures for auditory processing, verbal memory, and oral motor control. Narrative, oral tradition, and thematic correlation effected the unification of events in temporal and causal patterns. Myths presented imaginative models of the universe and a wider context for human life, especially myths of creation, social relationships, and life and death. Donald summarizes his finding: "Our genes may be largely those of a chimp or gorilla, but our cognitive architecture is not. And having reached a critical point in our cognitive evolution, we are symbol-using, networked creatures, unlike any that went before us. . . . Our minds function on several phylogenetically new representational planes, none of which are available to animals."[14]

Steven Mithen argues that the minds of our ancestors 100,000 years ago had specialized functions for particular cognitive domains, such as the natural world, social interaction, and the production of tools. The crucial transformation between 60,000 and 30,000 years ago was the achievement of "cognitive fluidity," which allowed inter-action among formerly separate domains. Mithen uses the analogy of a Medieval cathedral that started with a nave (generalized intelligence), to which were added separate chapels with no doors between them (specialized intelligences); only later did the nave and chapels become a single interconnected space. One form of cognitive fluidity, he suggests, was the imaginative capacity for metaphor and analogy in cross-domain thinking. The development of language and the cultural explosion in this period drew from all the domains. For example, the carving of an ivory figure of a man with a lion's head required technical ability and a combination of natural and social understanding. Burial sites give evidence of early forms of religion in ritual performance and belief in an afterlife.[15]

Ian Tattersall also defends the *uniqueness of humanity* in evolutionary history. He describes the intelligence of apes and their use of sign language. He traces the development of *Homo erectus* and his successors down to the Neanderthals who left no evidence of art or symbolic language. The art of the Cromagnons in the caves of southern France represents a huge leap, not simply an extrapolation of previous capacities. They created detailed images of animals and also mythical figures such as humans with animal heads. Some individuals were given elaborate graves with carved decorations and artifacts suggesting social stratification, burial rituals, and belief in an afterlife. The capacity for symbolic abstraction allowed wide scope for imagination in combining symbols in new ways. Tattersall argues that self-reflective insight made possible a larger range of choices, greater freedom of individual action, and a more rapid rate of cultural change. These new cognitive capacities combining reason and emotion emerged relatively suddenly and recently, a mere 30,000 years ago, though of course they were built on presymbolic capacities that had evolved over millions of years.[16]

We should note, however, that there has been an ongoing debate concerning the mental capacities of the Neanderthals. An anthropologist's interpretation of limited physiological data and ambiguous archaeological evidence may be influenced by initial assumptions and philosophical convictions that favor emphasis on either the similarities or the differences between Neanderthals and modern humans. As in comparisons with the abilities of chimpanzees, I find the case for human uniqueness convincing, though the gap between humans and other life-forms seems to be much smaller than has traditionally been assumed.

4. The Evolution of Religion

Let us consider the evolution of three basic features of religious life.

1. Ritual. Julian Huxley, Konrad Lorenz, and other ethologists have described animal rituals. Animals exhibit many formalized behavioral repertoires, such as the courtship or territorial rituals of animals and birds, which are genetically transmitted. One member of a species is programmed to respond to the ritual behavior of a second member, who can thus signal intentions and evoke appropriate responses. Some interpreters believe that human rituals may be supported by similar genetic and lower-brain structures, with strong emotional correlates, though the particular rituals are culturally learned higher-brain patterns.[17] Most anthropologists, by contrast, take ritual to be entirely transmitted by culture, with no specific genetic basis. They say that the most important human rituals help individuals and groups to cope with the major crises and transitions of life: birth, puberty, marriage, and death.[18]

Some anthropologists hold that ritual is the primary religious phenomenon from which other features of religion arose. They take religious beliefs to be later rationalizations of rituals, whose social functions are all-important. For example, almost every culture has initiation ceremonies in which the adolescent is brought into the adult world and the continuity of the social order is upheld. But other interpreters maintain that ritual has many dimensions, all of which are significant. Ritual is indeed community-forming, but it often takes the form of a symbolic reenactment of a story (myth). Some religious rituals, such as sacrifices and sacraments, are ways of relating to the holy. Rituals may be understood as vehicles for communicating with the divine, for expiating guilt, for celebrating and offering thanks, or for expressing grief and loss in a cosmic setting.[19]

2. Myth. Unique to humans is the need to live in a meaningful world. Myths or sacred stories are taken as manifesting some aspect of the cosmic order. They offer people a way of understanding themselves and of ordering their experience. They provide patterns for human actions and guidance for living in harmony with the cosmic order. These stories are often related to the experience of the sacred, and they point to a saving power in human life.[20]

Some stories refer to primeval times, the origins of the world and humanity, or the sources of human alienation, suffering, and death. Creation stories are found in almost all cultures. Other myths tell about the end of time or patterns of cyclical return or death and rebirth in the seasons and in human life. Still others are built around particular events or persons in the community's memory. Claude

Levi-Strauss and the structuralists find a common pattern in myths: the partial resolution of one of the basic contradictions or polarities in life, for example, life/death, good/evil, male/female, or culture/nature. The symbolic mediation of such conflicts helps people respond to individual and social stress and crisis, thereby aiding adaptation and social stability.[21]

3. Religious Experience. Eugene d'Aquili and Andrew Newberg claim that evolutionary history has wired the neural circuits of our brains for religious experience. Religion fulfills a basic human need to orient oneself in a wider framework of meaning, which can be provided by the experience of the unity of all things as well as by cosmic myths. These authors did brain-imaging studies of Buddhist monks and Franciscan nuns while they were deep in meditation. The studies show increased activity in the frontal lobe, which is the seat of attention even in the absence of sensory input. By contrast, activity decreased both in the right parietal lobe (associated with causal and temporal ordering as well as verbal and logical abilities) and in the left parietal lobe (associated with integrative, holistic, and spatial relationships). The reduction in temporal ordering activity evidently accompanies the loss of awareness of the passage of time reported by mystics in many cultures. The reduction in spatial ordering occurs in parallel with the sense of unity, loss of individual selfhood, and obliteration of all boundaries described by the mystics. Disciplined meditators report the experience of timelessness, oneness, serenity, and joy. They assert the ultimate goodness of reality and their loss of anxiety and fear.[22]

These findings might be interpreted as evidence that brain networks cause us to imagine the idea of God or a transcendent reality. Alternatively, one could say that the brain wiring developed as our ancestors responded to a transcendent reality. Every claim about reality, whether of a table, an electron, or another person's love, requires neural activity in the brain. The reality of the referent of our symbols can never be determined by examining the brain. On the other hand, the claims of the mystic inevitably go beyond the experience itself and involve interpretations influenced by language and cultural assumptions and concepts. Moreover, myth and ritual have been as important as religious experience in religious history, and mysticism is not the only form of religious experience. The numinous experience of awe, holiness, and the otherness of the sacred have been as common as the sense of unity and identity with the sacred. Ethical dimensions of religion have also been important. Both Catholic saints and Buddhist bodhisattvas are judged as much by their lives of love and compassion as by the intensity of their experiences.

These basic components—ritual, myth, and religious experience—seem to have been present in the earliest periods of human history as well as in nonliterate cultures today. But there were important developments during the centuries that Karl Jaspers has called *the axial period*, from 800 to 200 B.C.E., in five centers of civilization: China, India, Persia, Greece, and Israel. In this period parallel movements arose, from which have come all of the main world religions. Significant leaders stood out as individuals: Confucius, Gautama the Buddha, Zoroaster, Plato and Aristotle, the Hebrew prophets. Influential documents were written: the Tao Te Ching, the Bhagavad Gita, the Hebrew Bible, and so forth. (Of course, there were important earlier figures, such as Moses, and subsequent ones, including Jesus Christ and Muhammad; but Judaism, Christianity, and Islam are all derived from Hebrew monotheism, which took its distinctive form in the axial period.)[23]

The *world religions*, which have their roots in this period, share a number of features. Each tells of initial revelatory experiences that were interpreted and reinterpreted within particular historical contexts and cultural assumptions. All have sacred scriptures, which are extensively used in connection with worship, liturgy, and instruction. All have both specific moral teachings and more general ethical principles. They have faced common problems but sometimes responded to them in different ways. For example, in the earlier tribal period, religion had been strongly identified with the local community. The new traditions sought greater universality and the rational articulation of general principles, and they also allowed for more individuation. The self became problematic in a new way. The East frequently sought release from the self's bondage to suffering and anxiety through meditation and asceticism, while the West more often sought reorientation of the self through obedience to God.

Human Nature in Theology

Traditional Christianity has held that humanity was created in the image of God, fallen in original sin, redeemed in Christ, and called to love our neighbors and our enemies. We must examine each of these assertions in the light of evolutionary history.

1. Created in God's Image
The biblical statement that humanity is created "in the image of God" (Gen. 1:27) has often been taken to refer to particular human traits, such as rationality, moral agency, or the capacity for love. An

alternative view is that the image refers to the relation of human beings to God and indicates their potential for reflecting God's purposes. Human creativity can be seen as an expression of divine creativity. In all these interpretations the *imago Dei* expresses a positive view of the essential nature of human beings.[24]

There has been extended debate as to how much of the image was lost in the fall. The theologian Matthew Fox says that Genesis represents an "original blessing" of humanity, and that "original sin" was later given a central place only because Paul, Augustine, and their followers were pessimistic about human nature, leaving a powerful legacy of guilt among Christians.[25] Fox overstates his case, but it is clear that the Bible itself sees humanity as ambivalent, capable of both good and evil, rather than as fundamentally evil. "Thou hast made him little less than God, and dost crown him with glory and honor" (Ps. 8:5). We have remarkable capacities, which can be used creatively and compassionately. This basically positive appraisal of human nature has been characteristic of Judaism through the centuries.

The term *image of God* is used only in reference to human beings, suggesting *an absolute line* between humans and all other creatures. The claim to a unique status is reinforced by the subsequent verses, in which humanity is given dominion "over the fish of the sea and over the birds of the air and over every living thing that moves upon the earth." As we will see in chapter 6, the concept of dominion has been used to justify exploitative environmental practices, especially when other biblical themes such as stewardship of nature and celebration of nature have been ignored. But here we can note that the Bible itself combines the assertion of human uniqueness with the conviction that humans are part of a wider community of life and that we are all finite creatures of the Creator. The biblical view is ultimately theocentric rather than anthropocentric. Today our knowledge of evolutionary history is consistent with belief in human uniqueness, but it should lead us to give greater emphasis to the continuity and the similarities between human and nonhuman life than is evident in classical Christian thought.

In historic Christianity creation, the fall, and redemption were understood as separate and successive events which provided the narrative framework of a cosmic story. Today we can see them as three ongoing features of a single process of continuing creation, continuing fallenness, and continuing redemption.

2. Original Sin

According to a literal interpretation of the second chapter of Genesis, Adam and Eve were created in the garden of Eden, an idyllic paradise in which all creatures lived in harmony. Adam disobeyed God by eating from the tree of knowledge. Death and suffering came into the world as punishment for Adam's disobedience. But the evolutionary account tells us there was no primeval paradise. We probably are not descendants of a single pair of ancestors (though we may be descendants of a relatively small group, since in evolutionary history the formation of a new species has usually occurred when a small population has been isolated from the larger population of which it had once been a part). Suffering, conflict, and death long preceded the advent of humanity. Conflict has been an essential feature of evolution in which creatures compete with each other, and death was necessary for the appearance of new forms of life.

Today we can take the message of Genesis seriously but not literally. We can view Adam's story as an imaginative rendition of Everyman's journey from innocence to responsibility and sin. The story portrays the experience of anxiety, evasiveness, and a sense of guilt. Drawing from other biblical passages, we can understand sin not primarily as disobedience but as self-centeredness and turning away from God and the neighbor. It is a violation of relatedness that had destructive consequences for both the individual and society.

Paul Tillich identifies sin with three dimensions of *estrangement*. Sin is estrangement from other persons in self-centeredness and lovelessness. It is estrangement from our true selves in pursuing fragmented and inauthentic goals. It is estrangement from God, the ground of our being, in attempted self-sufficiency. For Tillich, estrangement, brokenness, and division can be overcome only in reconciliation, healing, and wholeness.[26] To Tillich's three forms of sin I would add a fourth: estrangement from nonhuman nature by denying its intrinsic value and violating our interdependence.

The doctrine of *original sin* is not found in the Old Testament (Hebrew scriptures) or in subsequent Judaism, but it is prominent in Christian history. Paul says that "sin came into the world through one man and death through sin" (Rom. 5:12), but he did not say that the body or sexuality are intrinsically evil; he lists sins of the spirit as prominently as sins of the body (Gal. 5:20). But Augustine held that Adam's sin was transmitted to his descendants through lustful acts of procreation. The official Roman Catholic position as articulated by Pius XII in 1950 is that the human body may have been the product of evolution from prehuman ancestors but the soul was a direct gift from God to the first humans, Adam and Eve, from whom all humanity is descended.[27] It is the universality of sin in our inheritance that makes redemption by Christ necessary. To the evolutionary biologist, however, both the assumption of a body/soul dualism and the inheritance of an acquired characteristic are likely to appear problematic (see chap. 4).

For many theologians today, original sin is not a biological inheritance from Adam but an acknowledgment that we have inherited *sinful social patterns* that preceded our own lives. The Hebrew prophets had of course spoken not only of the sins of individuals but also of the communal expressions of social injustice (Amos 1-4, for example). Reinhold Niebuhr has said that we are born into sinful social structures that perpetuate themselves in violence, racism, and oppression. Every group tends to absolutize itself, blind to the rationalization of its own self-interest. Niebuhr finds a profound ambivalence in the capacities for both good and evil in groups as well as individuals.[28] He suggests that democracy is possible because of the creative possibilities of human nature, but democracy is necessary because of the human tendency to abuse power.[29]

Philip Hefner proposes an *evolutionary interpretation* of the concept of sin. He identifies sin with the conflict between information in the genes and that in culture. Genetically based selfishness is in conflict with cultural sources of cooperation and altruism. Original sin consists in biologically based dispositions from the past that are not adaptive in the modern world.[30] The problem with this analysis is that it tends to make genes the source of evil and culture the source of good. I would argue that social injustice, violence, racism, and militarism are products of culture and social institutions and of individual decisions as much as of inherited genes.

Patricia Williams has written an interesting comparison of *sociobiology* and the doctrine of *original sin.* These two sources agree that behavioral dispositions can be transmitted sexually (genetically), though sociobiology traces this transmission back much further to prehuman ancestors. They agree that humans have inherited conflicting tendencies, among which we have only limited freedom to choose. But Williams says that we can make moral judgments and establish social rules that channel our innate dispositions in constructive rather than destructive directions. She insists that as symbolic creatures we can expand altruism by identifying ourselves with a wider circle, and can see all people as brothers and sisters under the fatherhood of God. She concludes that only the resources of a religious tradition can lead to a personal transformation that is built upon but goes beyond our genetic heritage.[31]

Authors in the eighteenth and nineteenth centuries believed in the perfectibility of humanity and the inevitability of progress in an Age of Reason. Events of the twentieth century have supported a more sober assessment of human nature. No event has more undermined such optimism than the depth of evil in the massacre of six million Jews in the Holocaust. This occurred, not in a primitive society, but in a nation of outstanding scientific and cultural achievements. Animals rarely kill members of their own species; their combat is often ritualized and stops short of serious injury. Yet among the human species, we have seen unprecedented violence, and a large fraction of the world's scientific and technological resources is devoted to improving military weapons, including weapons of mass destruction. The concept of sin is not outdated.

On the other hand, there is evidence from psychotherapy that *too negative a view* of human nature and too low an estimate of ourselves can be harmful. Guilt without forgiveness or self-hatred without self-acceptance seem to hinder rather than encourage love of others. Some theologians join psychologists in calling for a self-respect that is not self-absorption. Perhaps the goal is self-understanding and realism in recognizing both our creative and our destructive potentialities.[32]

3. The Role of Christ

The early Christians were convinced that in Christ *God had taken the initiative.* Preaching to Jewish listeners, they spoke of him as the Messiah, the deliverer whom Israel awaited. Writing to Greek readers, Paul used a different terminology: "In Christ God was reconciling the world to himself" (2 Cor. 5:19). John identified Christ with "the Word," the *logos* of Hellenistic thought, the principle of divine wisdom, which was now "the Word made flesh" (John 1:14).

For several centuries the church wrestled with ways of expressing its conviction concerning *the human* and *the divine* in Christ. The view of the Ebionites that Christ was a great teacher "adopted" by God for a special mission was rejected. Equally unacceptable was the opposite extreme, the Docetist claim that Christ was God incognito, merely disguised in the likeness of a man but not really human (and not really dying on the cross). The Nicene creed said he was "of one substance with the Father." The final formula agreed on at Chalcedon in 451 was "complete in Godhead and complete in manhood, two natures without division, confusion, or separation, in one person."

These *creedal formulas* served the negative function of ruling out unacceptable views. But they said nothing about how the "two natures" were related to each other. Moreover, they have often been interpreted in such a way that Christ's humanity was compromised (as an impersonal human nature without a human personality, or a human body without a human consciousness). The static Greek categories in which the doctrines were expressed, such as *nature* and *substance*, were familiar in the early church and in the Medieval world, but this framework of thought is both problematic and unfamiliar today.[33]

I submit that in reformulating ideas about Christ today we should keep in mind the intent of the classical doctrines but should make use of categories of *relationship* and *history* rather than of substance. On *the human side* of the relationship, we can speak of Christ as a person who in his freedom was perfectly obedient to God. Through his own openness to God, his life reveals God's purposes to us. He identified himself with God and did not obstruct or distort God's will. He was inspired and empowered by God. On *the divine side*, we can speak of God as acting in and through the person of Christ. Christ is thus God's revelation to us. What was unique about Christ, in other words, was his relationship to God, not his metaphysical "substance." We can speak of the unity between Christ and God and yet assert the presence of two wills. We have to think of what God did and also of what Christ did as a free human being. Without freedom and personal responsibility there would be no true humanity.[34]

I suggest, then, that in an *evolutionary perspective* we may view both the human and the divine activity in Christ as a continuation and intensification of what had been occurring previously. We can think of him as representing a new stage in evolution and a new stage in God's activity. Christ as a person (not just as a body) was part of the continuous process that runs back through *Australopithecus* to the early forms of life. He was also in the line of cultural and religious evolution that we have traced, and he was deeply formed by the ethical monotheism of Israel. Yet in his person and life and ideas, and in the community's response to him, he represented something genuinely new. We have said that in the sphere of culture, novelty is not the result of random mutations, and selection is not mainly a matter of physical survival; both are results of human freedom and decision.

But we can also view Christ as the product of a *divine activity* that has a long history. For millions of years there was the continuing creation of the nonhuman world, and then of humanity and culture, at an accelerating rate. In the great religious traditions of the world, and especially in the history of Israel, God's immanent creativity was increasingly focused, and individual persons were increasingly responsive. In Christ, both divine intention and human response allowed a more powerful revelation of God's nature than had occurred previously.

The Christian community believes that through Christ *reconciliation* may occur in our lives. If sin means estrangement from God, from ourselves, from other persons, and from the rest of nature, then reconciliation is also fourfold. Reconciliation with God takes place when repentance and forgiveness overcome guilt and when we know we are accepted despite our inadequacies. There is reconciliation with ourselves when healing and wholeness replace brokenness and fragmentation and when self-acceptance accompanies empowerment and renewal. There is reconciliation with other persons when we are released from self-centeredness, freed to love the neighbor and to take action for social justice.[35] Reconciliation with the rest of nature occurs when we recognize our common dependence on God and our continuing interdependence. If sin is indeed the violation of relationships, redemption is the fulfillment of relationships. For the Christian community the power of reconciliation and renewal is revealed most completely in the person of Christ.

There have been two main theological interpretations of Christ's death. In the *objective* interpretation, set forth by Anselm and dominant in Catholic thought and evangelical Protestantism, the cross is an expression of God's justice in relation to human sin. As a substitutionary atonement, "Christ died for our sins" by taking our place and undergoing the judgment we deserve. In the *subjective* interpretation, set forth by Abelard and dominant among liberal Protestants, Christ's self-sacrifice can inspire us to examine our own lives. Christ's teaching, life, and death are a revelation of God's love (more than of justice), and they can bring us to repentance. The transformation occurs in us as we ourselves accept God's forgiveness and love. The subjective view is more consistent with the understanding of Christ presented above, but at least some of the insights of the objective view can be combined with it.[36]

Geoffrey Lampe maintains that *God as Spirit* was present in the life of Christ. In the Old Testament, the Spirit was God active in creation and in human life, notably in the inspiration of the prophets. According to the Gospels, Christ received the Spirit at his baptism. The early church experienced at Pentecost an outpouring of joy and love, which they accepted as the gift of the Spirit. For them, the Spirit was closely associated with Christ, through whom they had come to a new experience of God. But Lampe points out that with the development of Trinitarian thought in the patristic period, the Spirit was no longer thought of as God's presence but as a separate being mediating between God and the world. The Holy Spirit was subordinated to the eternal Son, who was identified with the *logos* as agent of creation. It was said that the eternal Son assumed the general form of human nature—an idea that seems to compromise the historical individuality and the true humanity of Christ. According to Lampe, one God as indwelling Spirit was present in nature, the life of the prophets, Christ, and the early church—and can be present in our lives today.[37] Lampe holds that such a view brings together *creation* and *redemption* as a single continuous activity of God. Through the long evolutionary process God formed responsive creatures. But Christ was a focal point of God's activity and self-revelation, and he is for us the key to understanding the whole creative and saving work.

Roger Haight maintains that *God as Spirit* empowered Christ's human freedom rather than overpowering and controlling it. The indwelling of the Spirit is a personal presence that is dynamic and interactive, working from within to enhance freedom rather than to replace it. Similarly the experience of God as Spirit can empower our own lives. Christ is normative for the Christian community for whom he is the mediator of a new relationship to God. But God's love as revealed in Christ is universal, Haight says, so we must believe that the Spirit is at work in other religious traditions in their distinctive cultural contexts. "A Spirit Christology, by recognizing that the Spirit is operative outside the Christian sphere, is open to other mediations of God. The Spirit is spread abroad, and it is not necessary to think that God as Spirit can be incarnated only once in history."[38]

With this interpretation, I suggest, we can be loyal to the tradition in which revelation and renewal have occurred for us, without claiming that they cannot occur elsewhere. We can acknowledge divine initiative and human response *in other traditions*. We can respect the power of reconciliation wherever it occurs. This would lead to a path between absolutism and exclusivism, on the one hand, and relativism and skepticism, on the other. In a religiously pluralistic world, it would encourage genuine dialogue in which we can learn from each other without denying our indebtedness to our own traditions.

Can we imagine the Spirit at work even *on other planets*? The existence of fifty planets orbiting other stars has been reported, and the number will undoubtedly grow as observational techniques improve.[39] There are billions of stars in each of the billions of galaxies. In the previous chapter it was argued that evolutionary history on earth includes both lawful regularities and contingent events. It was suggested that design should not be identified with an exact predetermined plan, but rather with the emergence of new forms of order and a trend toward complexity, life, and consciousness. If even a small fraction of the planets in our galaxy, or in other galaxies, have conditions suitable for life, we would not expect extraterrestrial forms to look like us, with five fingers and five toes. But we would expect that some of them would be conscious, intelligent, and capable of personal relationships—capacities which we can believe are part of God's purposes for a universe that is far vaster in space and time and perhaps more diverse in its inhabitants than we have previously anticipated.

The existence of intelligent life on other planets would be problematic for persons who claim that Christ is the exclusive mediator of redemption. The inhabitants of distant planets could not even hear about Christ's life for thousands of years, and their lives might be very different from those of human beings. In his novel *Perelandra*, C. S. Lewis imagines a planet whose inhabitants do not need redemption because they have not fallen into sin. But the work of sociobiologists and theologians cited above suggests that conflicting emotions and ambivalent motives would likely be present wherever intelligent life has evolved. The same Spirit that was active in the life of Christ and in other religious traditions on planet Earth would surely be able to mediate God's love and the possibility of reconciliation in ways relevant to the inhabitants of other planets.

4. The Call to Love

Christ's ethical teachings include the injunction to "love your neighbor as yourself" and even to "love your enemies" (Matt. 22:39 and 5:44). This seems to be an impossible ideal if the sociobiologists are correct that we have been programmed by our genes to favor our genetic kin, and to cooperate reciprocally with our in-group, but to be aggressive toward other groups. The Christian tradition has of course recognized that the ideal of love is not easily achieved. We have seen that the concept of sin refers to self-centeredness and alienation from others, both individually and as groups. Radical love requires a fundamental re-orientation that is at the same time an individual decision and a response to God's love. "We love, because [God] first loved us" (1 John 4:19). In the knowledge that we are forgiven we may be enabled to forgive others.

Stephen Post has distinguished several *forms of love* in differing contexts. Love may be expressed as care toward a person in need, compassion toward a person in suffering, forgiveness toward someone who has acted harmfully, loyalty toward a friend, or joyful affection toward someone sharing an intimate relationship. In all these cases love affirms the value of other persons and seeks to empower rather than to control them. Love may involve significant risk to oneself (as in genuinely altruistic self-sacrifice), or it may involve mutuality (reciprocal benefits), but these are responses to particular circumstances rather than defining characteristics of love.[40]

Post sees human love as an extension rather than a denial of capacities present in our prehuman ancestors. Animals show a capacity for empathy (response to the emotions of others), and humans can combine this with greater understanding of the needs of others. Animal parents (mothers and in some cases fathers) protect and care for their offspring, and it is natural for human parents to do the same. Post suggests that within a Christian framework we do not need to deny the importance of the family and our responsibility for our immediate kin, but we should seek to widen the circle of our concern. Families today are often very inward-looking and do little to share their resources with others. The call to love, found in Christianity and in all the major world religions, can build on our more positive inherited tendencies and try to redirect the tendencies that are destructive in the context of current human life.

The Catholic theologian Stephen Pope argues that sociobiological evidence for the human predisposition to care for family and close kin should not be denied. He cites Thomas Aquinas's writings on "the orders of love," which include respect for one's parents, strong family ties, mutual friendship, and loyalty to the community. But the gospel calls us to extend these natural tendencies beyond our immediate community. In some situations the expression of love may require radical self-sacrifice and self-denial. But in most situations we have to combine our responsibilities to those nearest to us with our response to those in greatest need. By working for the public good we can overcome the individualism of modern life without expecting radical self-sacrifice or excluding mutuality and love of family and friends.[41]

People do indeed act from altruistic motives and some have made extraordinary sacrifices for the sake of persons to whom they were unrelated. In the village of Le Chambon in France during World War II, many families took great personal risks for months to hide Jewish children from the Nazi occupying forces until they could be taken to safety in Switzerland.[42] Other examples of altruistic behavior have been amply documented. But self-sacrifice should not be held up as a virtue in itself, especially when it involves submission to someone else. Wives have too often been praised for self-sacrificial sub-ordination to their husbands. Feminist theologians have pointed out that in a patriarchal culture women are likely to have too little self-esteem, not too much.[43] Love toward others is not incompatible with self-respect. Moreover, in confronting harmful actions of others both in the family and in the wider society, the call to love and forgiveness must be accompanied by the call to justice. Love of neighbor is expressed not only in individual actions but in working for more just social policies and institutions.

Genetic Determinism and Human Freedom

We have considered the role of genes in evolutionary history and some implications for a theological understanding of human nature. We turn now to studies of the influence of genes on human behavior today, starting with claims of genetic determinism based on knowl-edge of the human genome and studies of genetically related indi-viduals. Then the recent controversies over cloning, stem-cell research, and genetic modification are examined. The chapter closes with theological responses to these new applications of genetic knowledge.

1. The Human Genome

On June 26, 2000, U.S. President Bill Clinton announced completion of the mapping of most of the human genome by two research teams, one with federal funding and the other in an industrial laboratory. (A gene is a sequence of DNA bases that specifies a particular protein; a *genome* includes all the genes plus DNA segments that regulate gene expression plus some segments whose function is unknown.) Map-ping the human genome was indeed an amazing accomplishment, since it contains three billion DNA bases, comparable to the number of letters in a thousand thousand-page telephone books. The media announced that scientists had discovered "the blueprint for a human being." James Watson, the co-discoverer of DNA and the first director of the genome project, said that the project would tell us what it means to be human. "We used to think our fate was in our stars. Now we know that in large measure our fate is in our genes."[44] Walter Gilbert, also a Nobel laureate in molecular biology, has said that soon a person will be able to hold up a CD with his or her genome on it and say, "It's me."[45]

Such claims seem rather premature. We have no idea what most of the DNA segments do. A few diseases can be traced to a defect in a single gene, but the vast majority of human traits are polygenic, requiring the interaction of many genes. Each of us has 34,000 genes (compared to 19,000 in a roundworm), but we each have a million or so different proteins (far more than in a roundworm) because the proteins specified by human genes combine in complex ways. The task of tracing the functions of all these proteins has barely begun. Moreover, the image of the genome as a "blueprint" is misleading because it implies a predetermined outcome. It neglects the role of the wider environment in gene expression. In experiments on rats it has been shown that the neural circuits of their brains are not fully programmed but are affected by the richness of stimulation in the environment. The behavior of a cell is affected by distant influences through a host of chemical messengers. For example, hormones released when a person is under psychological stress can incapacitate the immune system, increasing susceptibility to a cold. Human identity and behavior are products of experience as well as genes.[46]

The thesis that we are determined by our genes is also *reductionistic* in claiming that the behavior of a larger whole is determined by the behavior of its component parts. In the previous chapter I argued that in complex organisms there is not only bottom-up causality but also *top-down causality* when wholes influence parts—not in violation of the laws governing the parts but by setting boundary conditions for their operation. I also referred to the *emergence* of behavior at higher levels of organization that could not be predicted from lower-level laws. The human self emerges in a biological process that is affected by genes but also by many other factors at higher levels. In human development, as in evolutionary history, selfhood is always social, a product of language, culture, and interpersonal interaction as well as genetic expression.

In some cases, however, a defect in *a single gene* is responsible for a life-threatening disease. Cystic fibrosis is caused by mutations in a specific gene for which a laboratory test has been developed. If both parents are carriers of the gene defect (without themselves having the disease), the chances are one in four that a child of theirs will contract it. If a young couple has a family history of the disease, they can be tested and with the help of a genetic counselor they can decide whether to conceive a child, adopt a child, or seek insemination by an anonymous donor. Alternatively the test can be carried out after conception on cells taken from the amniotic fluid, and the parents might decide to terminate the pregnancy. The test can also be done on a newborn child before the symptoms are apparent, and early therapy can greatly alleviate the impact of the disease. The genes responsible for other genetic diseases, such as Huntington's disease, have been identified but no therapy has been discovered. A healthy young adult can find out from tests that by midlife he or she will develop a painful and incurable disease. Some persons with a family history of Huntington's disease have sought such tests to help them in making life plans, whereas others have preferred not to know.[47]

Doctors and patients need to have access to the information provided by genetic screening, but the privacy of the patient must be protected to prevent abuse by other parties. Insurance companies and health-care providers have frequently dropped coverage of patients when they discovered that patients had a genetic defect, arguing that even in the absence of symptoms the patients had a "preexisting condition" that was grounds for exclusion. Patients might also be subject to genetic discrimination from employers who had access to genetic testing information. Such access is difficult to prevent when medical data are in computer files. Yet several legislative bills have been introduced in the U.S. Congress to protect patient privacy, and hopefully such legislation will pass in the future, despite the opposition of insurance companies.

Another version of genetic determinism arises from *behavioral genetics,* the study of behavioral similarities among genetically related individuals. The media have run headlines on "the discovery of the gene for alcoholism"—or for obesity, homosexuality, schizophrenia, etc. Studies of identical twins suggest that for many behavioral traits genetic factors account for roughly half of the variation. In one study comparing the brothers of 161 gay men, 52 percent of identical twins (sharing all their genes) were also gay, but only 22 percent of fraternal twins and 11 percent of adopted brothers were also gay.[48]

Other studies report that the percentage of African-Americans in prison is nine times that of the white population, and some commentators have concluded that genetic differences are responsible for *criminal behavior.* But this interpretation is highly questionable. Most if not all the racial differences in prison rates can be attributed not to genetic but to social factors such as higher unemployment among African-Americans or discrimination in arrest and conviction rates (six times as high for comparable crimes).[49] Controversial genetic studies have often been publicized by the media without the qualifications expressed in the original reports; later studies that failed to confirm the initial reports were seldom publicized. Studies of alcoholism are particularly problematic because it has several forms, each of which is affected by many genes as well as by personal history and cultural environment.

Genetic and cultural factors cannot be separated in any simple way. Even twins may seek out different environments, subcultures, and experiences that in turn affect their lives. Nature and nurture are always present together, and neither can be considered in isolation. Belief that human behavior is determined by genes undercuts motivation to reform social institutions that deal with poverty and crime. If our destiny is written in our genes, why waste money on social programs?

But even if we allow for the influence of environment as well as genes, we still have not included *human freedom*. Severe constraints are indeed imposed by nature and nurture. Genes establish a range of potentials and predispositions. Parents and social institutions present us with acceptable patterns of behavior. Freedom does not mean that our actions are uncaused or indeterminate but rather that they are the result of our motives, intentions, and choices, and not externally coerced. Freedom is self-determination at the level of the person. We are not passive stimulus-response mechanisms but selves who can envision novel possibilities and decide deliberately and responsibly among alternative actions. In the case of well-established habits, changes are not easily made, but they can occur if a person seeks a supportive context, as twelve-step programs for alcoholism have shown. We cannot choose the cards we have been dealt, but we can to some extent choose what we will do with them.

2. Cloning and Stem Cells

In 1997, Dolly the cloned sheep was born in Scotland. Her genes were identical to those of an adult sheep from one of whose cells the nucleus had been taken, injected into another sheep's egg, and stimulated electrically until it reverted to an undifferentiated state from which a complete new embryo grew. The motive of the experiment was to create sheep that could be used to produce new drugs for medical purposes.[50] Since then the technique has been improved and hundreds of animals have been cloned, including cows and pigs with superior characteristics sought by farmers. Both the clones and their offspring seem to be normal, though there have been some reports of premature aging and susceptibility to disease. I can affirm the motives and the intended consequences of animal cloning, assuming the risk of animal suffering or abnormality is minimal. Ethical issues will arise mainly in the context of social institutions: Who will have access to cloned animals? Will the companies that produced them control their availability through patents? What will be the affect on the lives of farmers and consumers?

Both the motives and the probable consequences of *human cloning* seem to me much more dubious. A father might want to clone an exact duplicate of himself—though of course this will not occur, since the clone will grow up a generation later in a different environment. A mother who has a daughter with a fatal illness might want to clone from her another daughter who could supply tissues or organs that could be transplanted without risking rejection—or who could "replace" her if she died. Such cloned children would be created not for their own sakes but to fulfill someone else's purposes. They would carry a heavy burden of expectations. It would be oppressive to know the life pattern of someone else with one's exact genes, even after acknowledging that the environmental contexts differ and personal choices remain. Until now, every human being in history (including twins and multiple births) has had two parents, and their particular genetic combinations have never occurred before. Each person's genetic inheritance is different from that of either parent. Cloning compromises the individuality of the child. The parent who controls both the genes and the home environment acquires unprecedented powers.[51]

The relational identity of the cloned child would be ambiguous and the family structure confusing. Should a child cloned from a woman be viewed as her daughter—or as her delayed twin sister? To be sure, a variety of new reproductive technologies have been developed in recent years, and gay and lesbian couples have worked out a variety of stable family patterns. But cloning presents a more far-reaching challenge to both individual fulfillment and enduring family relationships. Testimony at hearings of the National Bioethics Advisory Committee in 2000 stressed these ethical issues. In addition, many witnesses said that current cloning technology has unacceptable risks such as the possibility of deformed embryos, severely handicapped children, or delayed effects that might not show up for several generations.[52] The scientific community is virtually unanimous in holding that human cloning for reproductive purposes should not be attempted until there has been far more exhaustive research on animal cloning.

Late in 2001 a research company, Advanced Cell Technology (ACT), announced the cloning of the first pre-embryonic *stem cells*.[53] Stem cells have not yet specialized, and scientists hope that in the future they can be coaxed to specialize in building the distinctive tissues found in nerves, the heart, the kidney, and so forth. Experiments in England have shown that mouse stem cells can be induced to rebuild damaged nerve cells in the mouse's spinal cord. If stem cells are taken from a human patient, cloned, and then programmed for the tissue needed by the patient, they could be re-injected in the patient without encountering rejection by the immune system. In the past, a person whose spinal cord had been severed could expect to be paraplegic for life, but perhaps in the future stem cells could produce new nerve cells to repair the injury.

The researchers at ACT favor the cloning of human stem cells for such *therapeutic* purposes, but they are strongly opposed to their use for *reproductive* purposes. They point out that the cloned cells would be allowed to grow only to a small cluster of undifferentiated cells that could not exist outside the laboratory and would never be able to form a complete embryo. The stem cells would be taken from a pre-embryonic *blastocyst* before an *embryo* is formed two weeks after conception. (It is called a *fetus* ten weeks after conception, when rudimentary forms of most of the organs are present.)

Opponents of such research think that it is embarking on a "slippery slope" in which allowing therapeutic uses will make it more difficult to stop short of reproductive uses. However, legislation in the United Kingdom allows the therapeutic research but forbids implantation and reproduction. President George W. Bush issued an executive order in 2001 allowing federal funds to be used for research only on stem cell lines already present in laboratories, but it placed no restrictions on privately funded research.[54] I would myself favor the British approach, which allows research with either public or private funds for therapeutic but not for reproductive purposes. This would require a system of licensing and inspection and would make attempts to clone a human being a criminal offense. The decision about where to draw the line should not be made by researchers who have a financial interest in it but by legislators debating an important question of public policy.[55]

Some people have opposed stem cell research because they fear that some of the cells would be obtained by deliberate abortions. But there are other sources: existing cell lines, spontaneous abortions, and pre-embryos that would otherwise be destroyed because they are left over from *in vitro* fertilization (the fertilization of a woman's eggs by male sperm in a Petri dish, which usually creates more embryos than can be implanted). I would favor legislation allowing the growth of pre-embryonic blastocysts only up to fourteen days. Before fourteen days, twins can still be formed, so a stable individuality has not been established. In this period it is possible for stem cells to be induced to specialize before an embryo or fetus is formed. But many Christians (especially Roman Catholics and evangelicals) are strongly opposed to such a procedure because they believe that human life starts at conception and must from then on be accorded full human rights and protections. I respect the dedication to the sanctity of human life among those who hold this position and their concern to defend the powerless. But the belief that the soul is present from the time of conception was not the dominant view in classical Christian thought. Augustine's view that there is no soul until "quickening" (about 16 weeks) was widely held in the early church. This is the reason that fetuses that miscarried early in pregnancy were not baptized. Thomas Aquinas claimed that the soul can only be infused when there is a body ready for it—which he said would be at forty days for males and at eighty days for females.[56]

It is sometimes said that every fertilized egg has rights as a *potential* human being. But in normal intercourse several fertilized eggs are often created, of which only one is implanted. Are we to believe that those that are not implanted but excreted have souls that are lost forever? Every cell in the adult body contains the complete human genome, though much of it is inactive. If future technologies can induce adult cells to start a new cycle of life, every cell would be "a potential human being," but we could hardly accord full human rights to them all.

As an alternative to a body/soul dualism, I would defend a *developmental view* in which personhood is understood to develop gradually as the body does. Because this is an ongoing process, even a blastocyst should be treated with respect as a stage in a potentially ongoing process leading to personhood; it is not simply "disposable tissue." But its rights must be weighed against the rights and welfare of fully developed people. I suggested earlier that persons are intrinsically relational and social beings rather than self-sufficient individuals. A similar interdependence is evident after implantation, but not before. The growth of the embryo requires the growth of the placenta, genetic information from the mother's mitochondria, and a wide range of essential hormones and nutrients.[57] In the next chapter I will elaborate the concept of the person as a many-leveled unity rather than a dualism of body and soul. Such a view would allow the therapeutic use of pre-embryonic stem cells in the search for ways to alleviate human suffering, but it would insist on measures to prevent reproductive uses that might have harmful individual and social consequences.

Nevertheless, the developmental view of personhood draws no sharp lines and may therefore be particularly vulnerable to the "slippery slope" argument. Allowing the use of pre-embryonic stem cells might make it more difficult to control uses later in the developmental sequence. It might lead to greater callousness about sacrificing more fully developed human life. It might also strengthen the power of biotechnology companies that might later have a vested interest in reproductive as well as therapeutic uses. With a new technology, it may be easier to forbid everything or to forbid nothing than to make and enforce careful judgments about potential uses. This argument must be taken seriously, but it must be balanced against the great benefits of potential medical advances. It would at least suggest the need to have detailed regulatory procedures in place before allowing even limited uses.

3. Genetic Modification

Cloning duplicates all the genes in an existing genome. By contrast, genetic modification alters existing genes or introduces new ones. Modification may be aimed at correcting a genetic defect in either *somatic* (body) cells or *germ-line* (reproductive) cells. Another important distinction is between modifications designed to *correct a defect* and those designed to *enhance a desirable characteristic*.

1. Somatic Cell Therapy for Genetic Defects. Therapy on somatic cells affects only the individual treated without affecting future generations as germ-line therapy does. Research is currently directed at diseases that involve a single gene, especially those that are fatal. An experimental therapy can more readily be justified on a patient with a terminal illness, such as a cancer that has not responded to any other treatment. The defect responsible for cystic fibrosis has been located—an error in a single DNA triplet in the string of 1480 triplets that produces an important protein. Tay-Sachs disease and sickle-cell anemia are also promising candidates for future gene therapy. The hope is that, as genetic knowledge and techniques improve, it will be possible to add a missing gene or replace a defective one. Proposals for clinical trials of somatic cell therapies in the U.S. must go through several stages of review, from local ethics committees to committees at the National Institutes of Health. These reviews examine experimental trials in animals, provisions for confidentiality, the informed consent of patients (or their parents), and comparison with alternative therapies.

2. Germ-line Therapy for Genetic Defects. Somatic cell therapy would have to be repeated on individuals in successive generations, but germ-line changes would be passed on to future generations, which would be a more efficient use of medical resources. The prevalence of harmful genes would be permanently reduced. I would approve human germ-line therapy only under the following conditions. First, extensive studies of human somatic cell therapies similar to the proposed germ-line therapy should be conducted, if possible, to acquire data on the indirect effects of the genetic changes. Second, the effects of similar germ-line therapy in animals must be followed over several generations to ensure the reliability and long-term safety of the techniques used. Third, widespread public approval should be secured, since the therapy will affect unborn generations who cannot themselves give "informed consent" to the treatment. None of these conditions is currently even close to being met, so for the present only somatic cell therapy seems to me justifiable.

3. *The Selection of Desirable Genes.* All of the examples above are attempts to alleviate the effects of harmful genes. There are various methods for selecting or introducing desirable genes. The sex of a fetus can be determined from a sample of amniotic fluid, and the parents could choose the sex of their future child by selective abortion. In a patriarchal society, parents are likely to choose a son more often than a daughter, as has been happening in several Asian countries with serious social consequences. The combination of *in vitro* fertilization with germ-line intervention could be used to seek genetic improvements, though this is a more distant prospect. Parents would have a variety of motives for selecting particular characteristics, and they might project their own unrealized ambitions on their children. One could imagine a father who had hoped for a career in basketball trying to create a taller son. A working group convened by the American Association for the Advancement of Science concluded that human germ-line modification has not been shown to be safe and that its use for enhancement would widen inequalities and lead to the commodification of reproduction. They call for public regulatory mechanisms for both public and private germ-line research before it is pursued further.[58]

1. *Eugenics.* Eugenics is a social program for the improvement of society. One method is for the state to select the individuals who would be encouraged to reproduce. In Nazi Germany, a group of young women exemplifying "ideal Aryan characteristics" were chosen to be the mothers of an elite group of children. In the U.S., a deep-freeze bank has been established containing the sperm of men of outstanding mental or physical abilities, from among which women could choose to be artificially inseminated.[59] In the future, genetic engineering could be used to improve society, though we must not forget that most human characteristics are the product of many genes in complex interaction. There is no one gene for intelligence, much less for artistic ability or love and compassion.

Proposals for social eugenics—whether by selective breeding or germ-line intervention—appear very questionable. By what criteria would selection be made? All cultures want to avoid the suffering and death of severe genetic diseases, but less severe "defects" are culturally defined, and the specification of positive traits reflects even stronger cultural biases. Ideals of beauty, physical ability, and mental accomplishment vary historically. We must be cautious in imposing on future generations our images of perfection. We do inevitably impose our expectations on our children, and all education and social change impose our values on the future. But genetic changes are more irreversible and long-range and more uncertain in their unforeseen consequences.

In the film *Gattaca* biotechnology laboratories produce genetically improved children for parents who can afford them. The ruling class is served by a genetic underclass who came into the world through normal reproduction. Genetic advantages are added to the economic and educational advantages enjoyed by the privileged. The biologist Lee Silver expects "reprogenetics" (the combination of reproductive biology and genetics) to be the dominant factor in the human future. "In a society that values individual freedom above all else, it is hard to find any legitimate basis for restricting the use of reprogenetics. . . . The use of reprogenetic technology is inevitable. . . . And whether we like it or not, the global marketplace will reign supreme."[60] He predicts that this will end by creating two separate species, the "genRich" elite and the "Natural," who will be low-paid workers.

4. Theological Responses

What light does the Christian tradition throw on the ethical issues posed by cloning and genetic modification? There is no biblical verse that says, "Thou shalt not clone." Both the possibilities and the dangers of biotechnology are without precedent. But the biblical understanding of human nature can indirectly offer some guidance.

If we relied only on the belief that we are made *in the image of God,* we would stress human creativity and the potential benefits of biotechnology. Some theologians do in fact have an optimistic view of technology in general and expect it to liberate us from poverty, disease, and suffering. If we started from the doctrine of *original sin,* we would stress the potential dangers of the abuse of humanity's new powers. There is a long history of images of destructive uses of technology, from the Prometheus myth and the biblical Tower of Babel to modern novels such as *Frankenstein, 1984,* and *Brave New World.* But if we acknowledge our capacity for *both good and evil,* we would encourage creative uses of new technologies but insist on safeguards against abuses.[61]

The biblical tradition holds up a number of values relevant to decisions about genetic modification.

1. Social Justice. Justice is love expressed in the context of social institutions. Since the Hebrew prophets, the protest against injustice reflects the conviction that all people are of equal value in the sight of God. In considering any new technology we must ask who benefits from it and who profits from it. Who would have access to a new genetic therapy? What changes in healthcare delivery systems would broaden access? Biotechnology will increase further the power of pharmaceutical companies and biotech industries. How can a company be assured adequate profits, some of which are used for further research, without long-term patents that prevent other companies from providing desperately needed medications (such as those for AIDS/HIV) at lower cost? How can the need for industrial secrecy be combined with public accountability?[62] One form of original sin is the tendency of every group (including scientists with ties to industry) to rationalize its self-interest, so we cannot rely on self-regulation.

2. Human Dignity. The value of the individual is a recurrent biblical theme. It would lead us to defend privacy in genetic screening. It would also lead us to question the cloning of a human being to fulfill someone else's purposes—for example, the vanity of a parent or the medical needs of a sibling. We should resist the vision of "designer babies" who are viewed as technologically designed products. A future child must not become one more commodity that can be preselected and purchased. Commercialization and the technocratic model of manipulating life must not dominate human relationships. The biblical tradition has always valued the family, and we should question anything that undermines it, though we can be open to new forms of stable and committed relationship.

3. Unconditional Love. The use of genetic therapies to alleviate suffering can be seen as a form of love. But the worth of an individual does not depend on the absence of defect or disease. The search for "the perfect child" could affect attitudes toward people with disabilities. If parents think of an unborn child as a product for whose quality they are responsible, they may be unable to deal with their child's limitations. We will always need the courage to live with our own limitations and the compassion to accept those of others. Unconditional love and acceptance within the family and respect for all persons in society must not be compromised by efforts at genetic enhancement.

Some religious critics oppose all human genetic engineering as "tampering with nature." They assume that the world has permanent structures in accord with divine intentions. Human nature is said to be fixed and inviolable. But all medicine is an intervention in nature, even if it is aimed at fulfilling what one takes to be the true functioning of nature. Typhoid, after all, is part of nature. Moreover, in an evolutionary perspective, nothing—not even human nature—is fixed; all structures are changing. Still, we can at least meet these critics part way. Let us be grateful for the amazing human genetic heritage, aware of its complexity and fragility, and cautious about changing it when our knowledge is so limited. We should be wary of talk about redesigning humanity.

Other critics claim that we are "playing God" and usurping divine prerogatives when we try to modify human genes.[63] I would reply that creation was not completed once-for-all. I have suggested that God works through the continuing evolutionary process and through our lives today. Human beings are endowed with intelligence and creativity. We can be coworkers with God in the fulfillment of God's purposes. As coworkers we can cooperate with God in the continuing work of creation in nature and history.

Ronald Cole-Turner holds that God works through natural processes and can work through us if we choose to follow God's purposes. Cole-Turner is aware of the temptation to misuse our powers, as expressed in the traditional idea of original sin. He says that we must provide safeguards to limit the concentration of power in biotechnology industries. But genetic intervention can be a significant path to relief of suffering and a fulfillment of God's purposes. He maintains that we are called to participate in God's creative and redemptive work. Cole-Turner emphasizes the positive possibilities of genetic engineering, though he recognizes the dangers in germ-line intervention, especially in the enhancement of human traits.[64]

To sum up, we can acknowledge the power of genes in evolutionary history and in present human behavior. But as we look to the future, our choices—including our decisions about genetic modification—are not determined by our genes; they are influenced by our values and the ideals upheld in our religious tradition. Our future is a continuation of evolutionary history and also a continuation of God's project, in which human beings now have a crucial role because of the new powers acquired through science and technology. Only if we combine scientific knowledge with ethical sensitivity and political wisdom can we hope that these new discoveries will contribute to human fulfillment.

4

Neuroscience, Artificial Intelligence, and Human Nature

I hope to show that it is consistent with neuroscience, computer science, and a theological view of human nature to understand a person as a multilevel, psychosomatic unity who is both a biological organism and a responsible self. We can avoid both materialism and body-soul dualism if we assume a holistic view of persons with a hierarchy of levels. The themes I will consider are embodiment, emotions, the social self, and consciousness. In the first three sections I look at these themes from the standpoints of neuroscience, theology, and research on artificial intelligence in computers. I then examine some philosophical interpretations of consciousness. Finally I suggest that process philosophy can provide a conceptual framework for integrating these varied perspectives on human nature.

Neuroscience and Selfhood

Three themes in neuroscience (the study of the neural structure of the brain) are explored here: embodiment, emotions, and the social self. Research on the role of consciousness and the implications of such research for our understanding of selfhood are also considered.

1. Embodiment

Perception is an evolutionary product of bodily action. Humberto Maturana and Francisco Varela maintain that historically the needs and actions of an organism affected the type of perceptual system it developed. In a frog's visual system, certain neurons respond only to small dark spots— undoubtedly an advantage in catching flies. So, too, human neurophysiology evolved in parallel with distinctive human goals and interests.[1] Michael Arbib argues that perception is not passive reception of data but an action-oriented restructuring of the world.[2] Mental representations ("schemas") provide information relevant to actions that could be carried out under the guidance of perceptions, expectations, and goals. Other studies have shown that the development of vision in newborn cats is dependent on bodily movement.

The influence of biochemical processes on mental events is evident in many types of research on the effects of hormones, "mind-altering" drugs, and therapeutic medications. For example, Peter Kramer examines the use of Prozac in the treatment of depression. He defends its value in correcting chemical imbalances (especially in the neurotransmitter serotonin), but he concludes that the most effective therapy combines medication with consideration of traumatic experiences and psychosocial factors in the patient's personal history.[3]

The correlation of *brain sites* with particular cognitive functions can be studied by means of data on brain lesions or strokes occurring in human subjects or laboratory animals. Positron-emission scans can be used to monitor blood flow in small regions of the brain while the subject is carrying out an assigned cognitive task. Damage in a particular brain area has been found to prevent language acquisition without harming other skills. One patient with a brain lesion was able to write lucid prose but could not read it. Oliver Sacks describes patients who were unable to recognize faces but had no problem recognizing animals or objects.[4] Extensive research has been done on epileptic patients whose right and left brain hemispheres had been severed to control their seizures. Such patients might be able to follow instructions to pick up an object with the left hand, for example, but be unable to name it. But other mental functions seem to be widely distributed, and a given site may serve more than one function. Memory is distributed over many locations, with short-term memory differing markedly from long-term memory. Neural networks function globally and exhibit distributed properties. In all these cases, mental events are radically dependent on physiological processes at a variety of levels.

2. Emotions

Five approaches to the scientific study of emotions can be identified.

1. The Evolutionary Perspective. Darwin held that emotional behaviors are remnants of actions that were functional in evolutionary history. A dog's anger is evident in growling and baring the teeth, which embody a physiological readiness to act aggressively and signal such readiness to other creatures. A legacy of such behavior is seen when an angry person shouts and grimaces. Darwin claimed that a common evolutionary origin accounts for the universality of facial expressions of emotions in diverse cultures. Subsequent studies have found considerable cross-cultural consensus in identification of photographs of faces expressing six basic emotions: anger, fear, happiness, sadness, disgust, and surprise. Proponents of sociobiology and evolutionary psychology have offered hypotheses concerning the adaptive value of many behaviors associated with emotions.[5]

2. The Body-Response Perspective. William James held that emotions are internal perceptions of physiological processes in our own bodies—tense facial muscles, sweaty palms, and especially the effects of the autonomic nervous system, such as a pounding heart, faster breathing, and higher blood pressure. He claimed that emotions are the result (and not the cause) of physiological changes that we perceive directly. More recent studies of patients with spinal cord injuries showed that the feedback from internal organs does affect the intensity of a person's experience of emotions.[6]

3. The Cognitive Perspective. Whether an animal or a person flees in fear or fights back in anger may be partly instinctive, but it also reflects a cognitive appraisal of the situation and a judgment about its potential danger. Authors in this tradition talk about the meaning of events and the expectations and goals that people bring to their appraisals. They insist that emotion cannot be separated from cognition. They also go beyond the six emotions studied by the physiologically-oriented authors above to consider complex human emotions such as guilt, shame, and embarrassment, or anxiety in the face of uncertainty.[7]

4. The Social Perspective. Here the role of culture in the social construction of emotions receives strong emphasis. Emotional feelings and their expressions are shaped by cultural meanings learned in infancy and throughout life. Anger at another person is often related to the belief that the other person is to blame for an offending action. Guilt is an acknowledgment that one has violated one's own norms, whereas shame is the feeling that one is not worthy in the eyes of others. Historians and social psychologists have described the role of emotions as a means of social control (by shame and guilt, for example, in Puritan New England). Other studies suggest that when children learn words for emotions and culturally approved actions to express them, their emotional experience is itself affected.[8]

5. The Neural Perspective. Research on the physiological structures of the brain can help us understand the functioning of emotions. The amygdala and the hypothalamus in the limbic system have been shown to be crucial in several emotions. Joseph LeDoux uses elevated blood pressure and heart rate as indicators of the emotion of fear in rats when they hear a sound which they have previously been conditioned to associate with an electric shock. He finds evidence of *direct* neural paths from the auditory system to the amygdala that allow a rapid (evolutionarily valuable) response. He also finds *indirect* paths to the amygdala by way of the cortex that are slower but provide for interpretation and discrimination among sounds (as proposed by the cognitivists). LeDoux distinguishes between emotions as objective body responses and brain systems, on the one hand, and the subjective feelings associated with them, on the other, which he says are inaccessible to scientific study. [9]

These five approaches are often viewed as competing theories. Research does sometimes yield data that support one approach rather than another. I suggest, however, that they should be viewed as alternative perspectives using *different levels of analysis* that are not necessarily incompatible with one another. Emotions are multifaceted: they are at the same time adaptive mechanisms, bodily feelings, cognitive appraisals, social constructions, and neural processes. Nevertheless, we must go on to ask how these levels are related to one another.

Antonio Damasio has studied the relationships between *emotion* and *cognition* in people who have undergone damage in the prefrontal cortex. In a classic case, Phineas Gage recovered from a severe injury and retained his intellectual abilities but underwent a personality change in which he was unable to make decisions or observe social conventions. One patient with a prefrontal brain tumor was totally detached emotionally. When he viewed films depicting violence, he could describe appropriate emotional reactions but said he could not feel them, and he was unable to make decisions in daily life. Damasio argues that the cortex and limbic system work together in the construction of emotions. He suggests that both René Descartes and modern cognitive scientists have neglected the role of emotion in cognition. Damasio also holds that consciousness and continuity of identity are provided by self-representation and the construction of a narrative that includes personal memories and intentions. He describes the self as a many-leveled unity. "The truly embodied mind does not relinquish its most refined levels of operation, those constituting soul and spirit."[10]

3. The Social Self

Neuroscience provides many types of evidence concerning the social character of cognition in animals and humans.

1. Social Interaction. Leslie Brothers attached electrodes to the brain of a monkey watching videotapes of the face of another monkey. She found neurons selectively responsive to the other monkey's facial expression of emotions. She suggests that human infants are attentive to adult faces because they have been prewired by evolutionary history to respond to relevant facial signals. Human emotions are expressed and recognized within a socially constructed communicative system. Brothers insists that the mind is a social creation that cannot be understood by studying its neural basis alone. "I take the mind to be irreducibly transactional."[11] The person is part of a social-moral order, not something to be found in the neural account. Human actions are explained by reasons and historical narratives, not by physical and chemical causes. Through narratives we collaboratively create ourselves as persons as we enact our place in a social world.

Human language is of course a social product, even if the capacity for language is genetically based. Selfhood is intersubjective and relational, dependent on history and culture. The social world is internalized in the formation of one's self-image, which in turn affects one's interaction with other people. The whole field of social psychology is devoted to the study of phenomena that cannot be understood by analysis of individuals alone.

2. Memory and Narrative Construction. The stories we tell about ourselves as agents and subjects of experience are part of our self-identity. Children learn mental predicates and self-referential language as their parents ascribe intentions, desires, and feelings to them. We have a continuing identity as subjects, but memory is always an active reconstruction rather than simply a retrieval of information. We seek coherence and plausibility in our stories; narratives are revised and related to future goals and plans. The tragedy of Alzheimer's disease is the loss of the long-term memory that is required for self-representation. Sacks describes the case of "the lost mariner" with a brain lesion and memory loss, for whom art and music aided the reconstitution of a new identity.[12] The stories we tell about ourselves are also influenced by the stories present in our culture, including those of our religious traditions.

3. Cultural Symbol Systems. Human beings form symbolic representations of the self and the world that are always partial and selective. We seek meaning and order by seeing our lives in a wider context that is ultimately cosmic in scope. We identify ourselves with purposes and goals that extend beyond our own lives, temporally and spatially. Religious traditions have provided many of the symbols through which individuals integrate conflicting desires and make sense of their lives in a more inclusive context. In myth and ritual people participate in religious communities and share their historical memories and their experiences of personal transformation. These wider symbolic structures of order and meaning are indeed human creations, but I have argued that they are also responses to patterns in the world and in human experience, so they can be critically evaluated and revised.[13]

James Ashbrook and Carol Albright have proposed that models of ultimate reality can be found in neuroscience itself, particularly in Paul MacLean's idea of *the tripartite brain*.[14] The *upper brain stem*, which we share with creatures as far back as the reptiles, controls the basic life-support systems, such as breathing and reproduction. It offers an analogy to the image of God as the sustainer of the conditions for life. The *limbic system*, which we share with mammals, is the center of emotions that mobilize action and make richer forms of relationship possible, including empathy and care of the young. These qualities lead us to recognize emotion and social relationships as part of reality and to envision a nurturing and interacting God. The *neocortex* as it developed in primates and humans is the center of interpretation, organization, symbolic representation, and rationality. Damage to the frontal lobes affects the ability to prioritize, make plans, and pursue long-term goals. The left hemisphere is associated with verbal and logical analytical thought, and the right with visual, spatial, and holistic synthesizing thought. The activities of the neocortex would parallel the idea of a purposeful God who rationally orders and pursues goals.[15] (We should note that critics of MacLean have argued that the relationships between the three regions of the brain are more complex than he recognized, but a distinction of three functions of the brain might still provide analogies for envisaging God, as these authors propose.)

Ashbrook and Albright say that human beings seek meaning by viewing their lives in a cosmic and religious framework that is itself a *human symbolic construct*. But they go on to say that such symbol systems are not just useful fictions if they seek to interpret coherently the data of human experience. Moreover, the brain is itself part of the cosmos and a product of the cosmos, so its structures reflect the nature of the cosmos and whatever ordering and meaning-giving forces are expressed in its history.

4. The Role of Consciousness

Finally, let us consider some recent research on consciousness in human life that may be relevant to our concept of selfhood.

1. Unconscious Information Processing. Many instinctive responses and changes in the hormonal and autonomic nervous system occur without our being aware of them; our attention would be drastically overloaded if we had to keep track of all these changes. It has long been known that under hypnosis, and in subliminal perception, events of which we are not aware influence subsequent behavior. A variety of more recent experiments show the presence of unconscious information processing. *Blindsight* occurs in patients with a lesion in area V1 of the visual cortex. They say they are unable to see an obstacle in their path, yet they will act as if they see it and will walk around it. In another type of experiment carried out by Benjamin Libet, subjects were told to record the exact moment when they voluntarily initiated a finger movement. Electric impulses were detected in the brain (the so-called *readiness potential*) up to one-third of a second before the subject's decision, suggesting that brain processes occur before the subject is aware of them.[16]

Daniel Dennett reports experiments on *metacontrast* in which the image of a disc is followed after a very short delay by the image of a ring. Subjects say they have seen only the ring, yet they report that there were two stimuli. Dennett offers three possible explanations: the first stimulus was overridden before it entered consciousness; it entered consciousness but memory of it was then obliterated; or information from the first stimulus was reinterpreted in the light of the second one.[17] The experiment provides one more example of information processing that occurs without our being aware of it.

2. The Evolution of Consciousness. Simple organisms have a minimal *sensitivity* and responsiveness to the environment. If a one-celled paramecium finds no food at one location, it will use its coordinated oar-like hairs to move to another location. Perception of an elementary kind occurs when there is a selective response to information used to control actions. At somewhat higher levels *sentience* includes a capacity for pain and pleasure, which were presumably selected in evolutionary history for their contribution to survival. When a neural system is present, pain serves as an alarm system and an energizing force in avoiding harm. But continued pain may hinder action; even invertebrates under stress release endorphins and other pain-suppressant chemicals similar to those released in humans in response to pain, so it is reasonable to assume that they have at least some experience of pain.

Donald Griffin has studied the *mental abilities of insects and animals.* He associates consciousness with complex and novel behavior in unfamiliar circumstances. Bees can communicate the direction and distance of food sources and can distinguish between water, nectar, and a possible hive site; they do their waggle dance only when other bees are around, but they have limited ability to modify their behavior in new circumstances. Griffin argues that the versatile and goal-directed behavior of animals is evidence of thought, feeling, and conscious awareness. Animals imaginatively compare possible courses of action and anticipate their consequences. Comparison of mental representations of alternative actions allows for more rapid, diverse, and adaptive responses to a changing environment. But Griffin holds that self-awareness is present only in certain species of primates. When looking in a mirror, a great ape will touch a mark previously placed on its forehead.[18] As noted in the previous chapter, Terrence Deacon claims that primates have only a very limited capacity for symbolic communication. Teaching a few symbols to apes is a slow and arduous process requiring repeated rewards and punishments. The ability of primates to generalize and to follow logical rules (such as inclusion and exclusion) is impressive but far short of human capacities for language and abstract thought.[19] Such evidence would lead us to speak of *degrees of consciousness* rather than an all-or-nothing attribute.

3. *The Construction of the Self.* There are numerous versions of the thesis that mental activity is *modular.* Jerry Fodor's *Modularity of Mind* argues that the mind is a collection of relatively independent special-purpose modules.[20] Marvin Minsky's *Society of Mind,* making use of computational models, claims that the human mind is an aggregate of many small mindless components.[21] According to Michael Arbib, "the you is constituted by the holistic net of schema interactions in your brain." The coherence of the schema is achieved by their interaction and not by a central organizer.[22] William Calvin compares mental activity to a choir that works together, coalescing into a harmonious chorus without a conductor. A higher-order model of the self and the narratives in which it is represented serves to coordinate diverse subsystems.[23] Dennett argues that "multiple drafts" (alternative interpretive narratives) momentarily compete for attention below the level of consciousness, and we are aware only of the winning versions.[24]

Michael Gazzaniga, on the other hand, introduces a more centralized *coordinating system.* He finds that split-brain subjects will carry out an action with one brain hemisphere that uses information from a visual input to the other hemisphere of which they are not aware; they will then try to explain their action by some other reason, unrelated to the visual input. He postulates an Interpreter (in the left hemisphere, the main site of linguistic abilities) that monitors and integrates the unconscious activities and tries to make sense of them in relation to belief systems.[25] Robert Ornstein's *Multimind* proposes many small modules with specialized skills but also a governing self that links and coordinates these units.[26] A few brain researchers, including John Eccles, have continued to defend a dualism of mind and body in which the unity of conscious experience is an inherent property of mind; but this position has few adherents among scientists today.[27] There is thus considerable diversity among neuroscientists in their interpretations of modularity, but there is wide support for the idea that the unity of the self is achieved rather than given in the life of the individual.[28]

The Self in Theology

We have looked at the themes of embodiment, emotion, and the social self in the neurosciences. Let us consider the same three themes in the history of Western theological reflection, returning later to the question of consciousness.

1. Biblical Views

The biblical account of human nature may be summarized under three headings.

1. An Embodied Self, Not a Body-Soul Dualism. The Bible regards body and soul as aspects of a personal unity, a unified activity of thinking, feeling, willing, and acting. Joel Green writes: "It is axiomatic in Old Testament scholarship today that human beings must be understood in their fully integrated embodied existence."[29] According to Oscar Cullmann, "the Jewish and Christian interpretation of creation excludes the whole Greek dualism of body and soul."[30] In particular, the body is not the source of evil or something to be disowned, escaped, or denied—though it may be misused. We find instead an affirmation of the body and a positive acceptance of the material order. Lynn de Silva writes:

> Biblical scholarship has established quite conclusively that there is no dichotomous concept of man in the Bible, such as is found in Greek and Hindu thought. The biblical view of man is holistic, not dualistic. The notion of the soul as an immortal entity which enters the body at

birth and leaves it at death is quite foreign to the biblical view of man. The biblical view is that man is a unity; he is a unity of soul, body, flesh, mind, etc., all together constituting the whole man.[31]

According to the *Interpreter's Dictionary of the Bible,* the Hebrew word *nephesh* (usually translated as soul or self) "never means the immortal soul, but is essentially the life principle, or the self as the subject of appetites and emotion and occasionally of volition." The corresponding word in the New Testament is *psyche,* "which continues the old Greek usage by which it means *life.*"[32] When belief in a future life did develop in the New Testament period, it was expressed in terms of the *resurrection of the total person* by God's act, not the inherent immortality of the soul. Cullmann shows that the future life was seen as a gift from God, not an innate human attribute. Paul speaks of the dead as sleeping until the day of judgment, when they will be restored—not as physical bodies nor as disembodied souls, but in what he calls "a spiritual body" (1 Cor. 15:44). There were diverse strands in both Hebraic and Greek thought, and their influence on Paul's writing in the context of the Hellenistic world has been the subject of extensive discussion by biblical scholars.[33]

2. *The Role of Emotion.* "You shall love the Lord your God with all your heart, and with all your soul, and with all your mind" (Matt. 22:37). According to biblical scholars, these three terms—heart, soul, and mind—describe differing but overlapping human characteristics and activities rather than distinct faculties or components of the person. "The widely held distinction between mind as seat of thinking and heart as seat of feeling is alien from the meaning these terms carry in the Bible. . . . The heart is the seat of the reason and will as well as of the emotions."[34] Paul writes: "If I . . . understand all mysteries and all knowledge, and if I have all faith, so as to remove mountains, but have not love, I am nothing" (1 Cor. 13:2). Love is of course not simply a matter of emotion, because it involves intention and action. But clearly it is not primarily a product of reason. Some portions of the Bible, such as the Wisdom literature, express the outlook of the wise person reflecting on human experience. But in most biblical texts we are called to be responsible agents rather than simply rational thinkers. Sin is understood as a defect of the will, not of reason. In much of Greek thought, the basic human problem is ignorance, for which the remedy is knowledge. But in biblical thought it is our attitudes and motives that lead us astray.

3. *The Social Self.* In the biblical tradition, we are inherently social beings. The covenant was with a people, not with a succession of indi-

viduals. Some of the psalms and later prophets focus on the individual (for example, Jeremiah speaks of a new covenant written in the heart of each person), but this was always within the context of *persons-in-community*. Judaism has preserved this emphasis on the community, whereas Protestant Christianity has sometimes been more individualistic. In the Bible, we are not self-contained individuals; we are constituted by our relationships. We are who we are as children, husbands and wives, parents, citizens, and members of a covenant people. God is concerned about the character of the life of the community as well as the motives and actions of each individual.[35] The religious community shares a common set of sacred stories and rituals. Even individual prayer and meditation take place within a framework of shared historical memories and assumptions.

2. Medieval and Modern Views

Greek thought included a diversity of views of human nature and of these the greatest influence on early Christian theology was Plato's view that a pre-existent *immortal soul* enters a human body and survives after the death of the body. The Gnostic and Manichaean movements in the late Hellenistic world maintained that matter is evil and that death liberates the soul from its imprisonment in the body. The early church rejected Gnosticism, but it accepted the ontological dualism of soul and body in Neoplatonism and to a lesser extent the moral dualism of good and evil associated with it. Other forces in the declining Greco-Roman culture aided the growth of asceticism, monasticism, rejection of the world, and the search for individual salvation. Some of these negative attitudes toward the body are seen in Augustine's writing, but they represent a departure from the biblical affirmation of the goodness of the material world as God's creation.[36]

Thomas Aquinas accepted the Aristotelian view that *the soul is the form of the body*, which implied a more positive appraisal of the body. He said that the soul was created by God forty days after conception, rather than existing before the body. Aquinas gave a complex analysis of human nature and moral action that included an important role for emotions ("passions") in carrying out the good, which is known by reason.[37] Medieval theologians expressed a sense of the organic unity of a world designed according to God's purposes. Nevertheless the concept of an immortal soul presupposed an absolute line between humans and other creatures and encouraged an anthropocentric view of our status in the world, even though the overall cosmic scheme was theocentric. With few exceptions, the nonhuman world was portrayed as playing only a supporting role in the Medieval and Reformation drama of human redemption.

Descartes's dualism of *mind* and *matter* departed even further from the biblical view. The concept of soul had at least allowed a role for the emotions, as the biblical view had done. But mind, in the Cartesian understanding, was a nonspatial, nonmaterial "thinking substance," characterized by reason rather than emotion. Matter, on the other hand, was said to be spatial and controlled by physical forces alone. It was difficult to imagine how two such dissimilar substances could possibly interact. Descartes claimed that animals lack rationality and are machines without intelligence, feelings, or awareness.[38] The idea of the soul may have supported the dignity of the individual in Western history, but when understood individualistically it diverted attention from the constitutive role of the community in selfhood.

3. Contemporary Theology

An immaterial soul would be inaccessible to scientific investigation. Its existence could neither be proved nor disproved scientifically. But many *feminist theologians* today are critical of all forms of dualism for other reasons. They see in our culture a correlation of the dichotomies of mind/body, reason/emotion, objectivity/subjectivity, domination/nurturance, and male/female. Male is associated with mind, reason, objectivity, and domination, which are given higher status than body, emotion, subjectivity, and nurturance. Feminists decry the denigration of the body in much of Christian history; they seek a more positive evaluation of embodiment and a more integral view of the person.[39] *Environmentalist theologians* have criticized the soul-body dualism that postulated an absolute line between human and nonhuman life and thereby contributed to environmentally destructive attitudes toward other forms of life.

The theme of *the social self* is prominent among contemporary theologians. H. Richard Niebuhr defends "the fundamentally social character of selfhood," for "every aspect of every self's existence is conditioned by membership in the interpersonal group."[40] Niebuhr draws from George Herbert Mead and the social psychologists, who say that selfhood arises only in dialogue with others. We are not impartial spectators but members of communities of interpreters. The social context is also evident in the idea of *the narrative self*. Alasdair MacIntyre and others maintain that our identities are established by the stories we tell about ourselves. These stories always involve other people.[41] Advocates of "narrative theology" insist that our personal stories are set in the context of the stories of our communities. Religious beliefs are transmitted not primarily through abstract theological doctrines but through the stories told by the religious community that provide the wider framework for our own life-stories.[42] We have seen that the concept of the narrative self appears also in recent writings by neuroscientists.

Theologian Keith Ward maintains that soul and body represent not two entities but *two languages* for talking about humans. In the tradition of British linguistic philosophy, he considers the uses of differing types of language and their functions in human life, concluding that soul-talk functions to assert the value and uniqueness of each individual and to defend human openness to God. Language about persons is used to interpret the lives of embodied agents capable of responsible actions.[43]

A *two-language approach* is also adopted by several psychologists with strong theological interests. Malcolm Jeeves holds that "mind" and "brain" are two ways of talking about the same events. He cites Donald MacKay's claim that the first-person agent's story of mental events is complementary to the third-person observer's story of neural events, and not in competition with it. For Jeeves, science and religion also present complementary perspectives or ways of perceiving the world. Elsewhere he suggests that there are different levels of activity in the brain to which differing concepts are applicable, and that activities at higher levels causally affect activities at lower levels.[44]

Contemporary theologians have thus sought in various ways to recover the biblical themes of embodiment, emotion, and the social self, which we have seen are prominent in recent work in neuroscience.

Artificial Intelligence and Human Nature

We look now at research on computers and artificial intelligence (AI) and ask how it relates to neuroscience and our understanding of human nature.

1. Symbolic AI and the Computational Brain

AI research has a double goal: creating intelligent computers and understanding how the human brain functions. In an influential essay, Allan Newell and Herbert Simon maintained that a world of discrete facts can be represented by a corresponding set of well-defined symbols. They claimed that the relationships among symbols are abstract, formal, and rule-governed; symbols can therefore be processed by differing physical systems (natural or artificial) with identical results. They asserted that the brain and the computer are two examples of devices that generate intelligent behavior by manipulating symbols.[45] Symbolic AI tries to explain all cognition in terms of information, but it is not necessarily physicalist or reductionist because information is not reducible to the laws of physics.

Proponents of symbolic AI have made four assertions:

- *The Formalist Thesis.* Intelligence consists in the manipulation of abstract symbols according to formal rules.
- *The Turing Test.* A computer is intelligent if in performing tasks it exhibits behavior that we would call intelligent if it were performed by a human being.
- *Substrate Neutrality* (or *Multiple Realizability*). Software programs can be run on differing physical systems (neuron-based or transistor-based) with identical results.
- *The Computational Brain.* The human brain functions like a computer. In popular parlance, *mind* is to *brain* as software *programs* are to computer *hardware.*

Critics of formalism have said that human language and perception are *context-dependent.* Hubert and Stuart Dreyfus have portrayed the importance of common-sense understanding, background knowledge, and nonlinguistic experience in the interpretation of human language. Linguistic and perceptual understanding, they insist, are active processes, strongly influenced by our expectations, purposes, and interests.[46] They have also emphasized *the role of the body* in human learning. Much of our knowledge is acquired actively through interaction with our physical environment and other people. We learn to ride bicycles not by studying physics or by acquiring a set of rules but by practice. We use the skills of "knowing how" rather than the propositions of "knowing that." Such "tacit knowledge" cannot be fully formalized. In a child's development, growth in perception is linked to action and bodily movement. These authors see in the formalist thesis the legacy of a rationalism that goes back to Plato: the assumption that knowledge consists of formal rational relationships that exist independently of the body and the material world. They claim that formalism is a new kind of dualism in which software and hardware, like mind and body, can be analyzed independently.

Terry Winograd, whose programs for robots that could manipulate blocks were hailed as early successes in AI, subsequently repudiated formalism and stressed the importance of *individual and social life* in human understanding. He accepted Martin Heidegger's view that our access to the world is primarily through practical involvement rather than detached analysis. According to Heidegger, understanding is aimed not at abstract representation but at the achievement of our goals and interests. Our speech is communication for particular purposes, a form of action. Winograd also draws from Ludwig Wittgenstein, who insists that there is no private language or individual representation of the world, but only communication in contexts of social interaction. Language reflects our social practices, cultural assumptions, and "forms of life" in an interpersonal world. Winograd has redirected his own research and is working on the design and use of computers to facilitate human communication and social interaction, rather than to simulate individual human behavior in isolated domains.[47]

2. Learning, Robotics, and Embodiment

In most AI systems, discrete symbols that represent the world are processed serially. The development of *parallel distributed processing* (PDP), however, allowed many separate units to carry out operations simultaneously and to interact with each other without centralized control.[48] In task-oriented PDP networks, the system can be programmed to modify itself in successive runs, so that it learns by trial and error. One such network can be trained by an instructor to pronounce a text, converting various combinations of letters into a recognizable sound output from a voice synthesizer. The information is stored throughout the network, rather than by a one-to-one correspondence between separate data items and separate memory locations. Patterns develop in the whole without prior specification of the parts. If the learning procedure is repeated, the network will not end up with an identical circuit configuration.[49]

A further step is taken by Rodney Brooks and others in the design of robots that are *embodied, situated agents*. They are embodied in the sense that they can interact with the world through perception (using visual, auditory, and tactile sensors) and through action, and they are situated in particular environments. They have a minimum of central control; their architecture is decentralized in relatively independent units that interface directly with features of the environment in the generation of actions. New modules are added as incremental layers without disrupting existing modules.[50] Such robots learn by doing, not by manipulating abstract symbols. Their mechanical bodies are of course very different from our biological bodies; what they learn from their actions will differ from what we learn from ours.

Anne Foerst, who has degrees in both theology and computer science, has worked at MIT with the group designing the humanoid robot, Cog. She describes four of its characteristics:

- *Embodiment.* The group holds that human intelligence cannot be separated from bodily action or reduced to computational abilities. Cog has a "head" and "hands," which can move and interact with its environment.
- *Distributed Functions.* Small independent processing units activate local motor controls. Modular units with loose connections between them, rather than large centralized programs, allow greater flexibility in coordination and facilitate acquisition of new abilities without interfering with existing abilities.
- *Developmental Learning.* Like a newborn child, Cog learns visual-tactile (eye-hand) coordination from practice in grasping objects. Many of its capacities are developmentally acquired rather than preprogrammed.
- *Social Interaction.* Cog practices the equivalent of eye contact and is programmed to take into account some of the effects of its actions on people. These social features are at an elementary stage but are a goal of ongoing research.[51]

Foerst acknowledges that most of her colleagues think that *consciousness* is illusory and that they adopt a functionalist view of both human and robot capacities. Foerst herself says that there are "two stories" about human beings; computation provides models for only one of these stories. In our own lives we justifiably rely on our intuitive self-understanding. She calls for dialogue and mutual respect between theologians and computer scientists and recognition of the biases and limits of each discipline.

3. Socialization and Emotion in Computers

Recent work in robotics answers some of the objections raised against the symbolic AI program, but other questions remain in the comparison of artificial and human intelligence. The *process of socialization* in humans occurs over a span of many years. In computers, information processing is very rapid, but interaction with the environment takes considerable time. Robots might be socialized partly by being fed vast quantities of information; but if the critics of formalism are correct, participation in human culture and forms of life would require active interaction over a longer period of time. The Drey-fuses maintain that only computer systems nearly identical to the human brain and endowed with human motives, cultural goals, and bodily form could fully model human intelligence. That may be too strong a claim, but it points to the importance of culture as well as of body in human understanding and in any attempt to duplicate such understanding in machines.

The ability or inability of android artifacts to experience *emotions* has been a recurrent theme in science fiction, from Karel Capek's R.U.R. in 1923 to Commander Data in *Star Trek*. In the Stephen Spielberg film *AI*, an android which looks exactly like a real boy is programmed to love its adoptive mother. But it soon expresses unprogrammed emotions, such as jealousy and hatred towards the mother's real son. Most AI researchers claim only to simulate cognitive processes, and they hold that cognition is quite independent of emotions. Roger Schank writes:

> It would seem that questions such as "Can a computer feel love?" are not of much consequence. Certainly we do not understand less about human knowledge if the answer is one way or the other. And more importantly, the ability to feel love does not affect its ability to understand.[52]

Other authors hold that we can analyze the function of an emotion in evolutionary history and then try to construct an AI program that fulfills the same function. For example, the main behavioral function of fear is avoidance of danger, which could be programmed directly. Aaron Sloman has developed a computational theory of emotions (understood as dispositions to behave in certain ways). He says that computers could not experience feelings but could represent the cognitive components of emotions—for example, the external causes of anger and its relation to one's beliefs and ensuing actions.[53]

Rosalind Piccard's research is directed toward building computers with the ability to *recognize and express emotions*. Her goal is to facilitate communication between computers and humans. For example, a computer instruction program could slow down or offer further explication when it perceived expressions of frustration or anger in the user's face or heartbeat. A computer voice synthesizer might deliver a message with an intonation conveying an appropriate emotional tone. Piccard cites Damasio's work on the positive role of emotions in human cognition and suggests that emotional abilities would also contribute to computer intelligence. She remains agnostic, however, as to whether future computers might actually experience emotions. If they did, she says, their experience would differ greatly from ours, which is linked to physiological and biochemical processes unlike anything in computers. Some emotions, such as shame and guilt, reflect distinctive experiences of selfhood. Piccard says that we do not know enough about human consciousness to speculate on whether it could be duplicated rather than imitated in a computer. "Our feelings arise in a living and complex biological organism and this biology may be uniquely able to generate feelings as we know them. Biological processes may be simulated in a computer and we may construct computational mechanisms that function like human feelings, but this is not the same as duplicating them."[54]

4. Consciousness in Computers?

There are still enormous differences between *computers* and *brains*. A brain has 1,000 trillion neurons, each connected to as many as 10,000 neighbors; the number of possible patterns in interconnecting them is far greater than the number of atoms in the universe. Signals between neurons are not digital but are encoded in continuously variable properties, such as electrical potentials or neuron firing frequencies. Serial computers retrieve fixed information from local addresses; human memory is accessed through partial descriptive clues and is reconstructed in a more dynamic way. Gerald Edelman argues that parallel distributed processing in computer networks offers analogies to neural networks but that neurons and brains have many properties unlike those of computer chips. During embryonic development, for example, nerve cells connect to particular types of cells, but there is no exact prewiring such as computers require.[55]

Human beings are hierarchically organized, with many levels between the atom and the self; computers can indeed be built with hierarchical architecture, but the levels are less diverse and lack the degree of integration found at higher levels in organisms. Most computers are designed to be reliable by following precise algorithmic rules. To be sure, the final states of distributed networks in computers that learn from experience are unpredictable, but their potential for creative novelty seems rather limited. New knowledge from neuroscience will undoubtedly affect future computer design, but we should not underestimate the differences or the difficulties.

Is it conceivable that a future computer or robot could be *conscious*? A human infant develops by participation in a social and linguistic community. Events in the human mind are dependent on cultural contexts that extend far beyond the individual. The prospects for the socialization of robots are rather uncertain. But once we recognize that there are gradations of consciousness at different stages of an infant's development from a fertilized egg, and differing forms of consciousness in diverse animal species, we will not have to assume that consciousness in computers, if it is possible, will be like adult human consciousness. I suspect that it will turn out that conscious awareness requires forms of organized complexity or properties of neural cells and networks that have no parallels in silicon-based systems. I do not think we can exclude the possibility of conscious computers on metaphysical grounds, but there may be empirical grounds for the impossibility of computer consciousness. Because we know so little about the physical basis of human consciousness or the directions of future research in computer science, I am willing to leave this question open.

The mathematician and theologian John Puddefoot emphasizes the gap between computers and humans today. "To be regarded as something approaching the human, a computer would need to grow, feel pain, experience and react to finitude, and generally enter into the same state of mixed joy and sorrow as a human being. In particular it would need to be finite, aware of its finitude, and condemned one day to die."[56] On the other hand, he does not think we can set limits as to what might be possible in future computers. He speculates that with structures closer to those of living organisms, and with processes of evolutionary change within computers themselves, an artifact might conceivably produce its own forms of mind. Puddefoot adds that it was through evolutionary processes, after all, that God created human minds.

Our view of computers and robots, like our view of animals, will influence *our own self-understanding*. In relation to both animals and robots, interpretations that abolish sharp lines between human and nonhuman forms seem at first to be *a threat to human dignity*. But human dignity is not threatened if we recognize that future robots would be more than information processors and that they may share some of what we consider the higher human capacities. In the case of animals, our recognition of their similarities with humans has led to calls for respect for animal rights and for the inclusion of other life-forms in the sphere of moral consideration. In the case of robots a similar extension of moral status would be required. If they can suffer, as we believe animals suffer, we would have duties to minimize such suffering. Robots would also have moral responsibilities toward each other and toward humans.

In summary we can say that robotics joins neuroscience in underscoring the importance of embodiment, emotions, and socialization in human life and in acknowledging the problematic character of consciousness.

Philosophical Interpretations of Consciousness

Let us turn then to some philosophical interpretations of consciousness and its relationship to neuroscience and AI.

1. Eliminative Materialism

In *The Astonishing Hypothesis,* Francis Crick, codiscoverer of DNA, combines the presentation of data from the neurosciences with an explicitly materialist philosophy. He sees only two philosophical alternatives, a supernatural body-soul dualism or a materialistic reductionism. He equates dualism with religion, of which he is highly critical, unaware that many contemporary theologians have rejected dualism. The volume opens with this statement:

> The Astonishing Hypothesis is that "you," your joys and your sorrows, your memories and your ambitions, your sense of personal identity and free will, are in fact no more than the behavior of a vast assembly of nerve cells and their associated molecules. As Lewis Carroll's Alice might have phrased it: "You're nothing but a pack of neurons."[57]

On the scientific side, Crick is critical of cognitive scientists for relying on computational models and neglecting neural research. His book is mainly devoted to research on visual processing and awareness. He proposes that consciousness is a product of the correlation of diverse neural systems through electrical oscillations of roughly forty cycles per second. He suggests that the activities of various brain regions are coordinated when these oscillations synchronize the local neuron firings. He does not totally dismiss the subjective character of consciousness, but he does not think that it can be studied by science. "What may prove difficult or impossible to establish is the details of the subjective nature of consciousness, since this may depend upon the exact symbolism employed by each conscious organism."[58]

Dennett holds that "consciousness is the last bastion of occult properties and immeasurable subjective states." Qualia (phenomena as experienced) are vague and ineffable. The self is *a linguistic fiction* generated by the brain to provide coherence retrospectively among its diverse narratives. Dennett holds that "multiple draft" scenarios of which we are not aware compete for dominance. The self is the "center of narrative gravity" of these scenarios. It is a useful fiction that we create to provide order in our lives. But the unity and the continuity of consciousness are illusions. There is no enduring Cartesian observer who unifies our diverse perceptions. Nor is there a continuous "stream of consciousness," as posited by William James or James Joyce. There are only unconscious processes unified intermittently by a representation of the self that the brain repeatedly recreates from memories of the past and new scenarios in the present.[59]

Dennett describes *the intentional stance* as the strategy of acting as if other people had intentions. The ascription of intentions is predictively useful, but we do not have to assume that intentional states are ever actually present. Dennett claims that he is an instrumentalist or functionalist who judges concepts only by their usefulness in describing behavior, without asking about their status in reality. But he seems to accept a metaphysics of materialism when he asserts that neuroscience will be able fully to explain intentional action. He says that he is not a "greedy reductionist" who expects to explain all higher levels directly in terms of the lowest level, but that he is a "good reductionist," expecting to explain any level in terms of the next lower one.[60]

2. The Irreducibility of Consciousness

In replying to eliminative materialism, several philosophers have maintained that consciousness and subjectivity are *irreducible and inaccessible to science*. Thomas Nagel holds that consciousness cannot be understood from the objective standpoint required by science (which he calls "the view from nowhere"). Conscious and intentional states presuppose a particular viewpoint. Scientific theories cannot explain the experience of feelings or give an objective account of subjectivity. But science is not the only route to understanding; and in our practical life we inevitably attribute mental states to other people, and even to other species, though it is difficult to imagine what they are like. He cites evidence of the conscious inner life of animals but says that the experiential perspective can be understood only from within or by subjective imagination.[61]

Nagel does not defend a mind-body dualism but rather a *dual-aspect theory*. There is one set of events in the brain, of which mental concepts describe the subjective aspects and physical concepts describe the objective aspects. There is one substance with two sets of properties. Psychophysical laws connect the first- and third-person accounts, which are both valid. Personal identity is unified and linked to memory and intention as represented in first-person accounts. Nagel holds that mental aspects are present only in relatively advanced organisms.

Colin McGinn holds that consciousness is beyond our comprehension because of *the limitations of human knowledge*. Evolution has endowed every species with limited powers of understanding developed for practical purposes. The senses are useful for representation of the spatial world in which we live, but consciousness is not spatial. The brain can be studied as a spatial object; and its parts have spatial coordinates and predicates, such as size and shape. But the predicates of mental events are temporal rather than spatial. Knowledge of the correlations of phenomenal experience with physical data concerning the brain would not help us grasp the subjective character of consciousness, which cannot be described in the conceptual terms applicable to matter in space.[62]

McGinn believes that neural and mental events are correlated, but we cannot say how. Consciousness is a *causally emergent feature* of certain kinds of organized systems, but we cannot specify the necessary and sufficient conditions for consciousness to appear. Consciousness will remain an insoluble mystery, an intractable obscurity, because of our limited powers of comprehension. Both Nagel and McGinn seem to me correct in their critiques of reductionism, but I believe they underestimate the contribution of neuroscience to the study of patterns in mental events, even if science cannot capture the subjective feeling of such events.

3. Two-Aspect Theories

Owen Flanagan defends a *nonreductive naturalism* that draws from three sources: phenomenal first-person accounts, cognitive psychology, and neuroscience. He believes that the accounts can be correlated, though they have differing explanatory purposes. He takes seriously our conscious experience—our awareness of sensations, perceptions, emotions, beliefs, thoughts, and expectations. Flanagan describes neural correlates of visual experience, such as the neurons that respond to edges, shapes, colors, and motions, or the brain activities that are associated with fear and anger. But high-level concepts of the self are not expressible in neural terms. Human actions, for example, must be identified by the intentions that constitute them.[63]

Flanagan acknowledges that *the self is constructed*. It is not given to us as a single entity or a transcendental ego. The newborn gradually builds an integrated self with the help of parents and other people.

With maturation and socialization a distinct identity is formed, cast largely in narrative form in the stories we tell ourselves. The self is formed in active engagement with the environment and other persons. Our self-representations organize our memories of past events and our plans and aspirations for the future. Models of the self do not use concepts applicable to neurons, and they reflect our aims and values, which affect the choice of alternative patterns of action and human relationships.

In replying to Dennett, Flanagan agrees that the self is constructed but insists that it is not simply a useful fiction. Patterns of thought are real features of mental activity. The narrative self has *causal efficacy* as a complex and ever-changing self-representation. It causes people to say and do things; hence it has ontological and not merely linguistic status. Dennett had presented only two alternatives: either the self is an autonomous, enduring entity or else it is an illusion, a fiction that serves only instrumental functions. Flanagan offers a third: the self as a many-leveled reality that is constructed rather than given, in which activities at each level have some autonomy and yet are related to each other. This goes beyond Nagel's dual-aspect theory in arguing that there are causal relations between levels, rather than two perspectives on a single set of events. Flanagan does not share McGinn's pessimism about the contribution of neuroscience to our understanding of consciousness.

David Chalmers holds that *consciousness is irreducible* but argues that all other biological and psychological facts are determined by physical facts and are in principle explainable by physical theories. He holds that the cognitive sciences can provide reductive explanations for mental states considered as causes of behavior. Psychologists can even study awareness when it is viewed as access to information that is used to control behavior. They can give detailed functional accounts of memory, learning, and information processing, but they cannot say why these processes are accompanied by conscious experience, which is not defined by its causal roles. Phenomenal subjective experience is known firsthand in sensory perception, pain, emotions, mental images, and conscious thought.

Chalmers rejects materialism and functionalism and defends *a two-aspect theory*, which he also calls property dualism or a form of panpsychism. He proposes that *information states* are the fundamental constituents of reality and are always realized both *phenomenally* and *physically*. "We might say that the internal aspects of these states are phenomenal and the external aspects are physical. Or as a slogan: experience is information from the inside; physics is information from the outside."[64] A dog has access to extensive perceptual information, so we can assume it has rich visual sense experiences. A fly has rather limited perceptual discrimination and also a lower level of experience with fewer phenomenal distinctions. Simple information states would be realized in simple physical structures and simple phenomenal experiences. "It is likely that a very restricted group of subjects of experience would have the psychological structure required to truly qualify as *agents* or *persons*."[65]

Lynne Baker holds that neuroscience may provide the necessary and sufficient conditions for conscious events of a given modality but not the conditions for *particular reports of mental events*. We cannot expect neuroscience to explain the specific content of consciousness. No study of neuronal activity could confirm or disconfirm the report, "I realized that I believed Hal was trying to embarrass me." A person's belief that taxes are too high may be explained or predicted from other beliefs or events that psychologists and sociologists can study, but data at the level of neurons will not be illuminating. Beliefs are states of persons that help to explain their actions, not the interactions between neurons. Baker says that patterns of explanation at various levels indicate the reality of events at each level; she calls herself a metaphysical pluralist, not a dualist or a two-aspect monist.[66]

Of the three views in this section—eliminative materialism, the irreducibility of consciousness, two-aspect theories—it seems to me that the third is most consistent with human experience and with current theories in neuroscience. Process philosophy might be considered a form of two-aspect theory, but I suggest that it can better be described as dipolar monism.

Process Philosophy

The process philosophy of Alfred North Whitehead and thinkers influenced by him presents a coherent metaphysical framework within which many of the themes explored in previous sections can be brought together.

1. Dipolar Monism and Organizational Pluralism

Whitehead elaborated a set of philosophical concepts that emphasize becoming rather than being, change rather than persistence, creative novelty rather than mechanical repetition, and events and processes rather than substances. Whereas substances remain the same in different contexts, events are constituted by their relationships and their contexts in space and time. Whitehead and his followers hold that the basic components of reality are not one kind of enduring substance (matter) or two kinds of enduring substance (mind and matter), but *one kind of event with two phases*. In the objective phase a unitary event is receptive from the past; in the subjective phase it is creative toward the future. Every event is a subject for itself and becomes an object for other subjects.[67]

This philosophy is a form of *monism* because it insists on the common character of all unified events. "Dipolar" indicates an ontological claim, not merely an epistemological distinction, as some advocates of two-aspect monism propose. "Organizational pluralism" signals recognition that events can be organized in processes in diverse ways, as emphasized by Charles Hartshorne, who reformulated and extended Whitehead's ideas. All integrated entities at any level have an inner reality and an outer reality, but these take very different forms at different levels. Both the interiority and the organizational complexity of psychophysical systems have evolved historically.[68]

Looking at diverse types of system, Whitehead attributes *experience* in progressively more attenuated forms to persons, animals, lower organisms, and cells (and even, in principle, to atoms, though at that level it is effectively negligible), but not to stones or plants or other unintegrated aggregates. David Griffin proposes that this should be called *panexperientialism* rather than *panpsychism*, because for Whitehead mind and consciousness are found only at higher levels.[69] Only in advanced life-forms are data from brain cells integrated in the high-level stream of experience we call mind. Experience at different levels varies greatly; consciousness and mind were radically new emergents in cosmic history.

An *atom* repeats the same pattern, with essentially no opportunity for novelty except for the indeterminacy of quantum events. Inanimate objects, such as stones, have no higher level of integration; the indeterminacy of individual atoms in an inanimate object averages out in the statistics of large numbers. A *cell*, by contrast, has considerable integration at a new level. It can act as a unit with at least a rudimentary kind of responsiveness. There is an opportunity for novelty, though it is minimal. If the cell is in a *plant*, little overall organization or integration is present; there is some coordination among plant cells, but plants have no higher level of experience. But *invertebrates* have an elementary sentience as centers of perception and action. The development of a nervous system made possible a higher level of unification of experience. New forms of memory, learning, anticipation, and purposiveness appeared in *vertebrates*.

In *human beings,* the self is the highest level in which all of the lower levels are integrated. Humans hold conscious aims and consider distant goals. Symbolic language, rational deliberation, creative imagination, and social interaction go beyond anything previously possible in evolutionary history. Humans enjoy a far greater intensity and richness of experience than occurred previously. The human psyche is the dominant occasion that integrates and harmonizes the diverse streams of experience it inherits. Its continuity is achieved as the route of inheritance of a temporally ordered society of momentary events.

Process thinkers thus agree with dualists that *interaction* takes place between the mind and the cells of the brain, but they reject the dualists' claim that this is an interaction between two totally dissimilar entities. Between the mind and a brain cell there are enormous differences in characteristics but not the absolute dissimilarity that would make interaction difficult to imagine. The process view has much in common with two-language theories or a parallelism that takes mental and neural phenomena to be two aspects of the same events. But unlike many two-aspect theories, it defends interaction, downward causality, and the constraints that higher-level events exert on events at lower levels. At higher levels there are new events and entities and not just new relationships among lower-level events and entities.[70]

2. Embodiment, Emotions, and Consciousness

The themes in the neurosciences that were mentioned earlier are prominent in process philosophy.

1. Embodiment. Every unified event is portrayed as a synthesis of past bodily events. There are no events that have a subjective phase without a prior objective phase. This can be called an ecological, relational, or contextual philosophy because it holds that every basic unit is constituted by its relationships. Moreover, we experience the causal efficacy of our own bodies. The senses, such as sight, always have a bodily reference rather than simply transmitting information about the world. The body is the vehicle of relationality with other persons. Process thought defends the idea of *the social self,* which is a product of the interaction of embodied persons and not of disembodied minds.

2. Emotions. Process thought recognizes the importance of nonsensory experience and the perception of feeling in our own bodies. Consciousness and cognitive thought occur against a background of feeling. Whitehead writes: "The basis of experience is emotional. . . .

The basic fact is the rise of an affective tone originating from things whose relevance is given."[71] The technical Whiteheadian term *prehension* includes the communication of both conceptual and affective elements. The influence of one event on another is similar to the *communication of information*— including selective response by an interpretive system—but it includes an emotional component absent from most analyses of communication.

3. Consciousness. Whitehead says that consciousness first appeared in animals with a central nervous system as a radically new emergent. In human beings, most mental activity is unconscious. Consciousness occurs only in the last phase of the most complex occasions of experience, as a derivative byproduct of nonconscious experience. Self-identity consists in the continuity of processes most of which are below the threshold of awareness. Whitehead says that consciousness is "a late derivative phase of complex integration which primarily illuminates the higher phases in which it arises and only dimly illuminates the primitive elements in our experience."[72] It involves the unification of prehensions from the past and from the body with a new element: the contrast of past and future, the entertainment of possibilities, the comparison of alternatives.

4. A Hierarchy of Levels. Among process thinkers, Charles Hartshorne has developed most fully the idea of a series of levels intermediate between the atom and the self. He dwells on the differences between cells and mere aggregates, such as stones.[73] His holistic outlook directs attention to system properties that are not evident in the parts alone. Process philosophy has always insisted on contextuality and relationality. But it recognizes that various levels may be integrated according to different principles of organization, so their characteristics may be very different. In a complex organism, downward causation from higher to lower levels can occur because, according to process philosophy, every entity is what it is by virtue of its relationships. The atoms in a cell behave differently from the atoms in a stone, as cells in a brain behave differently from those in a plant. Every entity is influenced by its participation in a larger whole. Emergence arises in the modification of lower-level constituents in a new context. But causal interaction between levels is not total determination; there is some self-determination by integrated entities at all levels.

5. The Construction of the Self. Whitehead was influenced by William James, who held that there is no enduring self but only the stream of experience. Thought goes on without a thinker, or even a succession of thinkers aware of the same past. Continuity of identity, James said, is guaranteed only by the persistence of memory. He held that we each use a constantly revised model of the self to impose order on the flux of experience. Whitehead also holds that the self is a momentary construction, but he asserts that it is a unified complex process. The unity of self is a unity of functioning, not the unity of a Cartesian thinker. We have seen that this view—that selfhood is constructed—is consistent with recent neuroscience.

Yet I believe that Whitehead himself overemphasized the momentary and episodic character of the self. I have suggested that without accepting substantive categories we can modify Whitehead's ideas to allow for more continuity in the inheritance of the constructed self, which would provide for stability of character and persistence of personal identity.[74] Joseph Bracken agrees with my criticism of Whitehead and believes it can be remedied by emphasizing Whitehead's thesis that a temporal society maintains continuity among its momentary constituents ("actual occasions"). Bracken suggests "A much simpler way to preserve continuity among the discontinuity of successive actual occasions within human consciousness is to give greater importance to the Whiteheadian notion of a society as that which is created and sustained by a succession of actual occasions with a common element of form."[75] Bracken proposes that a society that endures over time can be understood as a "structured field of activity" for successive generations of events. "When applied to the Whiteheadian notion of the human self as a personally ordered society of conscious actual occasions, this means that the self is an ongoing structured field of activity for successive actual occasions as momentary subjects of experience."[76] Such revisionist or neo-Whiteheadian proposals can remedy some of the problems in Whitehead's writings while supporting his fundamental vision of reality.[77]

3. The Status of Subjectivity

My own view is very similar to the *emergent monism* defended by Philip Clayton and Arthur Peacocke.[78] We share a commitment to explanatory pluralism and the diversity of levels of explanation, including the distinction between reasons for human actions and causes of physical effects. We share a commitment to organizational pluralism in a hierarchy of many levels rather than a mind-matter dualism. We join in advocating contextualism, in which every entity is constituted by its relationships. Emergent monists also have a strong sense of the temporality and historical character of reality, and it would not be inconsistent for them to accept the Whiteheadian emphasis on momentary events and dynamic processes and the process critique of enduring substances. We agree that consciousness and mind are emergent new properties found only at high levels of complexity and that these potentialities were built into the lower-level components from the beginning.

However, process thinkers diverge from emergent monism by holding that at least a rudimentary form of subjectivity is present actually, and not just as a potentiality, in integrated entities at all levels. What are the reasons for such attribution?[79]

1. The Generality of Metaphysical Categories. In Whitehead's view, a basic metaphysical category must be universally applicable to all entities. The diversity among the characteristics of entities must be accounted for by the diversity of the modes in which these basic categories are exemplified and by differences in their relative importance. The subjective aspect of cells may for all practical purposes be ignored, but it is postulated for the sake of metaphysical consistency and inclusiveness. Mechanical interactions can be viewed as very low-grade organismic events (because organisms always have mechanical features), whereas no extrapolation of mechanical concepts can yield the concepts needed to describe subjective experience. New phenomena and new properties can emerge historically, but not new basic categories. Wings and feathers may evolve from other objective physical structures, but subjectivity cannot be described in physical terms. The subjective character of events is also important in process theology, because it provides one of the routes of God's influence on the world. The Whiteheadian analysis of causality allows for formal and final as well as efficient causes in all events.

2. Evolutionary and Ontological Continuity. There are no sharp lines between a cell and a human being in evolutionary history. Today, a single fertilized cell gradually develops into a human being with the capacity for thought. Process thinking is opposed to all forms of dualism: living and nonliving, human and nonhuman, mind and matter. Human experience is part of the order of nature. Mental events are a product of the evolutionary process and hence an important clue to the nature of reality. We cannot get consciousness from matter, either in evolutionary history or in embryological development, unless there are some intermediate stages or levels in between, and unless mind and matter share at least some characteristics in common.

3. Immediate Access to Human Experience. I know myself as an experiencing subject. Human experience, as an extreme case of an event in nature, is taken to exhibit the generic features of all events. We should then consider an organism as a center of experience, even though that interiority is not directly accessible to scientific investigation. To give a unified account of the world, Whitehead employs categories that in very attenuated forms can be said to characterize lower-level events, but that at the same time have at least some analogy to our awareness as experiencing subjects. Such a procedure might be defended on the ground that if we want to use a single set of categories, we should treat lower levels as simpler cases of complex experience, rather than trying to interpret our experience by concepts derived from the inanimate world or resorting to some form of dualism. It is of course difficult to imagine forms of feeling very different from our own, and we must avoid the anthropomorphism of assuming too great a similarity. Organizational pluralism allows for differences among levels and for the emergence of radically new phenomena, on which emergent monism rightly focuses attention.

In summary, process theology is supportive of the biblical view—which I suggested was consistent with the evidence from the neurosciences—that a human being is a multilevel unity, an embodied social self, and a responsible agent with capacities for reason and emotion. The dipolar monism and organizational pluralism proposed by process philosophy avoids the shortcomings of both dualism and materialism by postulating events and processes rather than enduring substances or entities. However, neither science nor philosophy—even when supplemented by data from the humanities and social sciences—can capture the full range of human experience or articulate the possibilities for the transformation of human life to which our religious traditions testify.

5

God and Nature: A Process View

In both Medieval and Reformation thought, God was said to be omnipotent, omniscient, unchanging, and unaffected by the world. According to the classical view, God is the absolute ruler of the universe. Every event is predestined in accordance with God's eternal will. This understanding of divine omnipotence is widely questioned today for four reasons set forth in the second section of the chapter: (1) the integrity of nature in science and in theology; (2) the problems of evil, suffering, and human freedom; (3) the Christian understanding of the cross; and (4) feminist critiques of patriarchal models of God. Such considerations have led many contemporary theologians to speak of God's voluntary self-limitation in creating the world. Most of these authors also hold that God participates in the suffering of the world. They reject the classical belief that God is unchanging and unaffected by the world.

The last section of this chapter explores the contribution of process theology in developing each of these four themes in a distinctive way. Process theologians hold that the limitation of God's power should not be thought of as a voluntary self-limitation, as if retaining omnipotence was an option that God decided to give up. The process view of the social character of all beings (including God) leads to an understanding of God's power as the empowerment of other beings rather than as power over them. This provides an alternative to both omnipotence and impotence by redefining the nature of divine power without denying its universal scope. The idea that God participates in the world's suffering is strongly supported by the process conviction that God is affected by events in the world. I will try to show that the God portrayed in process theology also has adequate resources for the redemptive transformation of suffering.

Historical Background

As background for the contemporary discussion, let us look briefly at biblical and Medieval views of God's relation to the world.

1. Biblical Models of God

Models are analogies drawn from one domain of experience to interpret events in another domain of experience.[1] The Bible includes a variety of models of God. In Genesis, God is portrayed as a purposeful designer imposing order on chaos. Other biblical passages picture a potter forming an object (Jer. 18:6, Isa. 64:8) or an architect laying out the foundations of a building (Job 38:4). God is envisaged as Lord and King, ruling over both nature and history. In relation to Israel God is a liberator delivering the community from bondage and a judge dedicated to righteousness and justice. In relation to the individual God is a careful shepherd and a forgiving father. In the New Testament, God creates through the Word (John 1), a term that brings together the Hebrew idea of divine Word active in the world and the Greek view of word (*logos*) as rational principle. For John, the purpose of creation was made known in Christ, the Word incarnate. Here is a rich variety of models, each a partial and limited analogy, highlighting imaginatively a particular way of looking at God's relation to the world.

The potter and craftsman analogies assume the production of a completed, static product. They seem less helpful in thinking of an ongoing, dynamic evolutionary history. The image of God as gardener is more promising, though it occurs rarely in the Bible (for example, Gen. 2:8), perhaps because the Israelites wanted to distance themselves from the nature gods of the surrounding cultures. The model of father is used for God's relation to persons, but there is also a fatherly care for nature (for example, the birds and lilies in Matt. 6:26, 28-30). God as mother was a rare image in a patriarchal society, but it appears occasionally (for example, Isa. 49:15 and 66:13). The parental analogy is usually drawn from a parent nurturing a growing child rather than from procreation and birth. This seems a particularly appropriate image of God's relation to the world. The wise parent allows for an increasing independence in the child while offering encouragement and love. Such an image can maintain a balance between what our culture thinks of as masculine and feminine qualities, in contrast to the heavily "masculine" monarchial model of omnipotence and sovereignty.

In chapter 1, I discussed the biblical image of God as Spirit. Here the analogy is the distinctive vitality, creativity, and mystery of the human spirit, the active person as a rational, feeling, willing self responding to other persons and to God. The Hebrew word for spirit (*ruach*) is also used for breath and is identified with life. The Spirit is God active in the world, whether in the initial creation (Gen. 1:2) or continuing creation (Ps. 104:30). The Spirit also represents God's activity in the worshipping community and in the inspiration of the prophets. I suggested in chapter 3 that Jesus Christ was inspired by the Spirit, as appears in the account of the baptism.[2]

2. Medieval Theology

In the Middle Ages, biblical and Aristotelian ideas were brought together, especially in the writings of Thomas Aquinas that have been so influential in later Catholic theology. The biblical model of God as king and ruler was elaborated into formal doctrines of divine omnipotence and omniscience. The dominant model was that of the absolute monarch ruling over his kingdom, though other models were also present. A similar view of God was prominent in the Reformation, particularly in Calvin's emphasis on divine sovereignty and predestination.

In the classical doctrine of *divine omnipotence,* God governs and rules the world in providential wisdom. All events are totally subordinate to God's will and power. Foreordination was said to involve not only foreknowledge but also the predetermination of every event. Both Medieval Catholicism and Reformation Protestantism held that God intervenes miraculously as a direct cause of some events, in addition to the more usual action of working through secondary natural causes. This was taken to be a strictly one-way relation: God affects the world, but the world does not affect a God who is eternal and unchanging.[3]

The exclusion of all temporality from God's nature seems to have been indebted mainly to Greek thought. Plato had pictured a realm of eternal forms and timeless truths, imperfectly reflected in the world; the perfect was the unchanging. Aquinas argued that God is *impassible,* unaffected by the world. God loves only in the sense of doing good things for us, but without passion or emotion. God's being is wholly self-sufficient and independent of the world and receives nothing from it. Since God knows all events in advance and controls every detail, divine knowledge is unchanging; in God there is no element of responsiveness. In the last analysis, the passage of time is unreal to God, for whom all time is spread out simultaneously. All of this seems to contrast with the dynamic God of the Bible, who is intimately involved in Israel's history and responds passionately to its changing situations.

To be sure, other themes qualified the Medieval and Reformation image of divine sovereignty. God's control was never sheer power, for it was always the power of love. Dante ends *The Divine Comedy* with a vision of God as "the Love that moves the Sun and other stars."[4] Classical theism indeed emphasized transcendence, and God was said to act occasionally by supernatural intervention from outside nature. However, divine immanence was also defended. In the classical view, God is preeminently present in the incarnation, the sacraments, and the life of the church.

God's Self-Limitation

Four themes are prominent in recent criticisms of the classical understanding of divine omnipotence.

1. The Integrity of Nature

With the rise of modern science, nature was increasingly seen as a self-sufficient mechanism in which God could act only by intervention from outside in violation of the laws of nature. Of course, if God created the laws of nature, God is presumably free to abrogate them or to make use of higher laws. Moreover, many laws of science are now known to be probabilistic or statistical, describing the way a system usually behaves when no additional influences (natural or supernatural) from outside the system are introduced. Nevertheless, dependable regularities are characteristic of most domains of nature, and science itself would not be possible without them. Moreover, the long and wasteful history of evolution suggests that God does not intervene frequently or coercively. If God is active in the process, it must be in a more subtle way that always builds on the structures and activities already present. If there is any role for God, it must be by working with the powers of existing creatures rather than by overruling them.

Several recent authors have said that their accounts of divine action do not involve violations of the laws of nature or divine intervention in gaps in the scientific account (the "God of the gaps," who retreats as each gap is closed by advances in science). Instead they have tried to show how new scientific concepts either permit divine action or suggest analogies for it. George Ellis holds that God determines the indeterminacies left open by the laws of quantum physics. As indicated in chapter 2, John Polkinghorne proposes that God acts by the communication of "pure information" at the exquisitely sensitive bifurcation points described in chaos theory, without violating the conservation of energy. Arthur Peacocke argues that God acts by "top-down causality" similar to the top-down influence of higher levels within an organism on its lower-level components (by setting boundary conditions and constraints rather than by violating lower-level laws). He also speaks of God's action in the world as an extension of the way in which larger wholes can affect changes in their parts within organisms. In all these cases God is seen as working subtly in cooperation with the structures of nature rather than by intervening discontinuously. [5]

There are also theological reasons for affirming the integrity of nature. The intelligibility, rationality, and dependability of nature can be interpreted as plausible evidence for an intelligent creator, though not as a conclusive argument. It would be a deficient design if God had to correct it frequently. Michael Welker has commented on the passage in Genesis: "Let the waters bring forth swarms of living creatures. . . . Be fruitful and multiply. . . ." (Gen. 1:20-22). He says that such passages do not portray the "absolute dependence" of creatures on God, as often claimed, but point instead to the cooperation of the creatures in divine creativity.[6]

Authors in the Thomistic tradition have tried to reconcile divine omnipotence and the integrity of nature. They say that God as primary cause works omnipotently through the secondary causes of nature. All events in the world are said to be the product of a divine plan in which everything has been predestined in accordance with God's will. God's primary causality is on a completely different level from the chain of secondary causes, which is complete and without gaps at its own level. This interpretation of natural causes as instrumental to God's absolute governance of nature was also defended by John Calvin, and more recently by Karl Barth and Austin Farrer, among others.[7] Critics reply that evil in the world and human freedom are incompatible with the assertion that all events are ultimately determined by God. I will suggest that process thought offers a detailed critique of both natural determinism and divine determination. It articulates roles for God and for natural causes in every event while rejecting traditional ideas of divine omnipotence.

2. Evil, Suffering, and Human Freedom

Pain and suffering are widespread in nonhuman nature. In evolutionary history, increased capacity for pain was apparently a concomitant of increased sentience and was selected for its adaptive value in providing warning of danger and bodily harm. The behavior of animals gives evidence that they suffer intensely.[8] Predators live off their prey, and many organisms consume organisms lower in the food chain as a source of complex organic molecules. Evolutionary history has involved struggle and competition in which the vast majority of species have become extinct. Holmes Rolston gives an example of a tragic dimension in nature. A white pelican lays its eggs two days apart. The later, smaller chick is allowed to survive only if the larger chick has succumbed at an early age. The usual fate of the smaller chick is to be attacked and fed to the larger one or pushed out of the nest.[9]

To be sure, what is harmful to the individual may benefit the group or the larger system. Even in nonlinear thermodynamic systems, disorder is a condition for the emergence of new forms of order. Death is a necessary feature of evolution in which changes occur between generations and finite resources can support only limited populations. The predator's prey contributes to the ecosystem, and the back-up chick contributes to future generations of pelicans. Rolston says that nature is "cruciform" when suffering serves a wider purpose and new life arises from the old. In "suffering through to something higher," nature offers a pattern that is fulfilled in the suffering Redeemer and the suffering of God with and for creation.[10]

With the emergence of higher levels of sentience and consciousness in evolutionary history, the capacity for greater suffering and the capacity for greater enjoyment were inescapably linked together. In human life, suffering contributes to moral growth, as Paul asserts (Rom. 5:3). Courage would be impossible without danger and temptation. The suffering of others calls forth our sympathy and compassion, and undeserved suffering can have a redemptive effect on other people. Moreover, the free choice of good would not be possible without the alternative choice of evil. John Hick, following Irenaeus, sees the world as an opportunity for moral development and "soul-making." The injustice of undeserved suffering, he says, can be rectified in the afterlife. Hick sees the presence of evil and suffering as evidence of God's self-limitation. He also holds that God withholds divine power to provide the "epistemic distance" that allows us to respond freely to divine love rather than being overwhelmed and coerced into belief.[11]

I question whether moral development alone can justify the extent and pervasiveness of suffering in human life, or the depths of human evil, brought home to me anew by a recent visit to Auschwitz. Some people do indeed gain courage and strength in encountering suffering, but others are broken and embittered by it. Voluntary self-limitation exonerates God from direct responsibility for specific instances of evil and suffering, but presumably God is ultimately responsible for them. How would we view a human father who withheld measures that could have prevented the protracted suffering of a person with AIDS or a prisoner at Auschwitz? A human father does not of course establish the ground rules for ongoing life, but the analogy may give us pause in claiming that divine omnipotence is only temporarily withheld. By contrast, process thought suggests that the limitations of divine power are the product of metaphysical necessity rather than voluntary self-limitation.

Moreover, human freedom seems to be excluded by both biological determinism and divine omnipotence. As noted in chapter 3, comparisons of twins (having identical genes) with non-twin siblings (sharing half their genes) and adopted children raised together (with few shared genes) show that in the case of many behavioral traits roughly half of the similarities are genetically inherited. This does not prove that human freedom is illusory, but it does suggest that our decisions are severely constrained by our genes. We can make choices only within a limited range of possibilities.[12] In other studies, damage to particular areas of the brain and changes in the balance of chemicals in the brain have been shown to affect particular mental abilities dramatically. The dependence of mental and spiritual life on biological processes calls into question the traditional dualism of body and soul. Freedom can be defended only if we can show that a human being is at the same time a biological organism, an embodied self, and a responsible agent.

The experience of choice seems to be an indelible feature of firsthand personal experience. Even the philosopher or scientist who defends determinism assumes in daily life that other people are responsible for their actions. In this chapter, however, we are primarily concerned with the threat to human freedom from divine determination rather than from biological determinism. Moral choice is frequently called for in the biblical literature. "Choose this day whom you will serve" (Josh. 24:15). Paul wrestles with the paradox of human freedom and divine grace. "I worked harder than any of them, though it was not I, but the grace of God which is with me" (1 Cor. 15:10). "Work out your own salvation . . . for God is at work in you" (Phil. 2:12-13). Paul also recognizes that true freedom requires not only the absence of external constraints but the resolution of internal conflicts: "For I do not do the good I want, but the evil I do not want is what I do" (Rom. 7:19). Both Paul and Martin Luther held that human sin results in a "bondage of the will" from which we can be liberated only by our acceptance of God's love.

Writers in the Thomistic tradition have tried to reconcile human freedom with divine foreknowledge and predestination. Human freedom occurs in the realm of successive temporal events; God desires our free response, not coerced obedience. But God transcends time; divine knowledge is eternal and unchanging. God knows the future, not as it is unpredictably produced by human choices and worldly causes, but as it is determinately specified by divine decree. Within the world, an act is uncertain before it takes place, but for God there is no "before." All time is present to God simultaneously.[13]

I would reply that this solution implies that time is unreal to God. Divine interaction with human life would be more like the staged performance of a prepared script than an intimate involvement in an ongoing relationship. Here I join those who say that God is omniscient in knowing all that can be known, but this does not include choices that are unknowable until they are made. The "free-will defense" in theodicy asserts that the price of human freedom is the possibility of the choice of evil. Polkinghorne has used the term *free-process defense* to refer to divine self-limitation in the nonhuman domain.[14] I would prefer to speak of creativity rather than freedom in nature apart from humanity, but clearly similar issues are at stake concerning God's power and knowledge in human and nonhuman domains. Process theologians have insisted that if God's experience is temporal, then human freedom implies limitations in God's power and knowledge of the future.

3. The Christian Understanding of the Cross

The Bible presents diverse images of God. In some parts of the Hebrew scriptures, God is the Lord mighty in battle in defense of the chosen people. Isaiah is overwhelmed by the majesty and mystery of God in his vision in the temple (Isaiah 6). But God is also compared to a grieving husband, strong in judgment but tender in forgiveness toward an unfaithful wife (Hosea 1-4). Later chapters of Isaiah portray Israel as God's "suffering servant," whose suffering can redemptively affect other nations (Isaiah 53), a role which early Christians believed was fulfilled in the person of Jesus Christ.

Paul writes that Christ "did not count equality with God a thing to be grasped, but emptied himself, taking the form of a servant. . . . and became obedient unto death, even death on a cross" (Phil. 2:6-8). In this passage the Greek work *kenosis* (self-emptying) refers to the self-limitation of Christ's power, but it also refers to the self-limitation of God's power in allowing Christ's death. Christians have understood the cross on the one hand as the result of Christ's choice of the path of self-sacrificial love in decisions throughout his life—from the temptations in the wilderness at the start of his public career to his free decision and faithful response in the garden of Gethsemane near its end. But they have also claimed that in the incarnation and in Christ's death God participated in human suffering and showed the power of redeeming love. The cross thus represents the nature and will of God as well as the fully human decisions of Christ. We would expect such a God to act kenotically in creation as well as in incarnation.

Among modern writers, W. H. Vanstone has shown that a characteristic of authentic love is its vulnerability, and he concludes that this would be true for God as well as for humanity:

Thou art God; no monarch Thou

Thron'd in easy state to reign;

Thou art God, Whose arms of love

Aching, spent, the world sustain.[15]

In *The Creative Suffering of God,* Paul Fiddes presents a critique of traditional ideas of God's self-sufficiency and immutability. Fiddes gives a sympathetic discussion of process philosophy, though in the end he argues that God's temporality and vulnerability are better expressed by the Trinitarian interaction within the life of God.[16]

We have seen that in the Bible the Holy Spirit is God's activity in nature, in the experience of the prophets and the worshipping community, and in the life of Christ. In many biblical passages the Spirit is said to work from within to renew, inspire, empower, and guide—all of which are noncoercive actions, of which the dove at Christ's baptism is an appropriate symbol. Some images of the Spirit (as wind or fire, for example) suggest a stronger influence, but the active participation of the individual is still required. There are thus distinctive biblical grounds for defending a kenotic theology.

4. Feminist Critiques of Patriarchal Models

Feminist theologians are concerned that the virtues that are taken to be "masculine" in our culture (such as power, control, independence, and rationality) are held to be superior to the "feminine" virtues (such as nurturance, cooperation, interdependence, and emotional sensitivity). The cultural priority of the first set of virtues can be seem as both a cause and an effect of male dominance in Western social structures. Patriarchal models of God in Christian thought are the product of a history in which both church leadership and theological reflection have been controlled almost exclusively by men.[17]

Feminist authors have given attention to the caring and nurturing aspects of human nature—and of God—that have been less highly respected historically than the characteristics of power and justice. Feminine images of God not only support the self-respect of women but allow stronger representation of neglected aspects of the divine nature. Feminist writings often emphasize the Spirit as the only non-gendered member of the Trinity, or they turn to the feminine expression of God as Sophia (Wisdom).[18] Such images may seem to diminish God's power, but they can better be understood as expressing a different form of power—not power as control over another person but power as empowerment of another person. Creative empowerment is not a "zero-sum" game (in which one person loses something when the other person gains it) but rather a "positive-sum" game (in which both parties can gain).

However, feminist authors have pointed to the dangers when Christ's self-sacrificial death is used to justify self-sacrifice on the part of women. Women have too often been given the role of "suffering servant," and have themselves accepted this role, enduring abuse with patience. Elizabeth Johnson says that voluntary suffering for the sake of a greater good may indeed be admirable—as when civil disobedience on behalf of social justice results in imprisonment. But many women are involuntary victims of sexual and domestic violence and lack the courage to resist. Johnson maintains that self-respect and self-affirmation are not incompatible with love of others and can contribute to mutually fulfilling relationships. She points out that the literature of psychotherapy shows that the capacity to care for others correlates more frequently with self-acceptance than with self-abnegation or low self-esteem.[19]

Joanne Brown and Rebecca Parker argue that Christ's death must never be used to justify suffering. According to the substitutionary atonement theory, developed by Anselm, the Son was obedient to the Father and "died for our sins," taking the punishment we deserve. Brown and Parker criticize the idea of a propitiatory sacrifice which vicariously satisfies the retributive demands of divine justice. Such a theory also endorses obedience and sanctifies suffering, which are not messages women need to hear. Brown and Parker see some advantages in the "moral influence theory" (following Peter Abelard), which says that Christ's undeserved suffering brings us to repentance and acceptance or forgiveness; this interpretation emphasizes divine love more than justice. But even this theory does not encourage victims to resist those that oppress them. These authors insist that Christ did not deliberately seek suffering. He suffered when his message of radical love challenged the prevailing structures of religious and political power. Both divine and human love are active in resisting and overcoming suffering, not in welcoming it.[20] We must take these caveats from feminist authors into account in any formulation of kenotic theology that emphasizes self-sacrifice.

Process Theology

Whitehead himself is explicit in rejecting the monarchial model of God as "imperial ruler." Instead, he speaks of God as "the fellow-sufferer who understands."[21] He defends "the Galilean vision of humility," in which God offers "tender care that nothing be lost." While the "primordial nature" of God is the source of all possibilities, the "consequent nature" of God is influenced by the world.[22] Extending Whitehead's analysis, Charles Hartshorne offers a critique of traditional concepts of divine impassibility and immutability. He defends "dipolar theism," in which God is temporal and changing in interaction with the world but eternal in character and purpose.[23] According to both authors, God shares our suffering by participation in the world, and this in turn affects us, as another person's sympathy can affect us in human life.

In describing the unfolding of every event, Whitehead includes the influence of past events, the ordering of potentialities by God, and an element of novelty. This is a God of persuasion rather than coercion. Such a conceptuality is particularly helpful in representing the evocative character of divine love in human life. Divine love would not be relevant to the inanimate world if the world were conceived as a deterministic mechanism. But it is relevant to nature seen as a hierarchy of levels with downward causation and the communication of information from higher to lower levels, or to the view of nature set forth in process philosophy.

We have seen that, in place of materialism or mind/matter dualism, process thought presents a pluralistic two-aspect monism in which all events have a subjective and an objective aspect but a pluralism of diverse levels of organization. This view should be called *panexperientialism* rather than *panpsychism* since experience is postulated at all levels in integrated events (but not in unintegrated aggregates like rocks or loosely integrated structures like plants). Mentality and consciousness are said to occur only in the last phase of complex processes in higher organisms.[24] God's influence on separate cells or molecules is minimal though not totally absent—which would be consistent with the long and slow course of evolutionary history before higher levels were present. Let us ask how the process understanding of divine power differs from the versions of kenotic theology described above.

1. Voluntary Self-Limitation or Metaphysical Necessity?

Process thought is distinctive in holding that limitations of divine knowledge and power arise from metaphysical necessity rather than from voluntary self-limitation. In analyzing omniscience, process authors claim that if temporal passage is real for God, and if chance, novelty, and human freedom are features of the world, then the details of future events are simply unknowable, even by God, until they occur. It would make no sense to say that God might have had knowledge of the future but set aside such a capacity. Similarly, process thinkers present a view of reality in which divine omnipotence is in principle impossible.

Charles Hartshorne elaborates a metaphysics in which all beings, including God, are inherently social and interactive. Every being has passive and receptive capabilities as well as active and causally effective ones. No being can have a monopoly of power or effect unilateral control. It is not as if the presence of the world limits God's otherwise unlimited power, since any valid concept of God must include sociality and relationality. Hartshorne says that in some aspects God is temporal and affected by the world but in other aspects God exemplifies classical divine attributes. God alone is everlasting, omnipresent, and omniscient (in knowing all that can be known). God is perfect in love and wisdom and unchanging in purposes and goals. God offers an initial aim to every entity and orders the world through cosmic laws that limit but do not exclude creaturely freedom. God's power is universal in scope. It "influences all that happens but determines nothing in its concrete particularity."[25]

To say that the limitation of God's power is a metaphysical necessity rather than a voluntary self-limitation is not to say that it is imposed by something outside God. This is not a Gnostic or Manichean dualism in which recalcitrant matter restricts God's effort to embody pure eternal forms in the world. If God's nature is to be loving and creative, it would be inconsistent to say that God might have chosen not to be loving and creative. We cannot say that God was once omnipotent and chose to set aside such powers temporarily. If behind God's kenotic actions there was an omnipotent God who refrained from rescuing the victims of pain and suffering, the problem of theodicy would still be acute, as noted earlier. Hartshorne objects to divine omnipotence on moral as well as metaphysical grounds. Within a social view of reality, persuasion has a higher moral status than coercion, even if it entails greater risk of evil and suffering. He says that God does all that it would be good for a supreme being to do, though not all that it would be good for other beings to do for themselves.[26]

2. The Adequacy of God's Power

The limitation of divine power in process thought may make the problem of the existence of evil more tractable, but does it leave God powerless to overcome evil? Hartshorne goes further than Whitehead in portraying God's ability to transform evil redemptively and to empower people with courage to resist evil. The process theologian Daniel Day Williams writes:

> I think Dr. Hartshorne is right in stressing also the coercive aspects of religious experience. To worship God in dependence on his holiness does transform the self, far beyond its conscious intent and understanding. When we oppose God we discover the boundaries of our action, which are starkly there, and the consequences which are visited upon us whether we will or no. There are large coercive aspects in the divine governance of the world.[27]

Williams in turn goes beyond Hartshorne in defending divine initiative in history and in the person of Christ. He holds that for God, as for human beings, "to love is to be vulnerable," but he maintains that in some respects God is invulnerable. "God's love is absolute in its integrity forever. In this sense it is invulnerable."[28] Events in the world may threaten the fulfillment of God's purposes, but God's being is not threatened. God remains faithful to the creation.

Williams cannot accept the divine monarch who controls all things and guarantees victory over evil, but he also cannot accept the divine aesthete who can only take up the tragic elements of life into a larger and more harmonious picture, as some passages in Whitehead suggest. Between these extremes Williams portrays the divine companion whose influence is transformative and redemptive.[29] He describes a client who finds that a psychotherapist can hear his story without being threatened by it. Such sharing of suffering is a form of acceptance and communication. Healing can arise from the sharing and reinterpretation of suffering. So, too, God's participation in Christ's suffering and in ours is "God's act of self-identification for us, his way of communication to us, and his healing power among us."[30] Moreover, God's action in Christ can empower us to cooperate in the alleviation of the suffering of others. For Williams, divine love, like human love at its best, seeks neither power over others nor power-lessness, but reciprocity and mutual empowerment.

Anna Case-Winter proposes a synthesis of process and feminist thought. She argues that the strength of process thought lies in its conceptual framework and in its critique of the intellectual adequacy of classical views; she draws particularly from Hartshorne's analysis of divine power. She says that the strength of feminist theology, on the other hand, is its attention to the experience of people in particular life situations and social contexts. Feminists have been more aware of the social and political consequences of theological ideas and the way concepts of God have been used to legitimate patterns of domination and oppression. But process and feminist authors share a commit-ment to starting from experience and to using holistic, social, rela-tional, and organic models of reality. Both groups understand God's power not as overpowering but as empowering. Case-Winter suggests that God is like a mother who empowers a child *in utero* and in sub-sequent life by working with other powers, not by displacing them. Such views of divine power would encourage forms of human power that are consistent with freedom, responsibility, and an ethics of sol-idarity with the oppressed.[31] Other writers have also noted the simi-larities between feminist and process thought.[32]

3. The Beginning and the End

Whitehead wrote before scientific evidence of the Big Bang was avail-able. He held that God and the world have always coexisted, and that God creates by working with what already exists. Whitehead postu-lated an infinite sequence of "cosmic epochs" differing significantly from each other.[33] Subsequent process thinkers have generally fol-lowed him in defending an infinite temporal past, and some have suggested that cosmic epochs might be identified with successive cycles of *an oscillating universe,* expanding and contracting, with a Big Crunch before each Big Bang. Process authors have said that God is always creative and social, bringing order and novelty out of chaos. They have criticized the doctrine of creation *ex nihilo* for overemphasizing transcendence, and they have defended continuing creation, which gives greater prominence to divine immanence.[34] But recent evidence suggests that our universe may be expanding too rapidly for it to slow down in the future and then eventually contract.

An alternative to an oscillating universe is the theory of *quantum vacuum fluctuations,* which is supported by many cosmologists today. Quantum theory permits very brief violations of energy conservation. In the laboratory, a vacuum is really a sea of activity in which pairs of virtual particles come into being and almost immediately annihilate each other. Perhaps our universe started from an enormous fluctuation that rapidly expanded, following the scenario of current inflationary theory. Our universe would be one of many coexisting universes that expanded too rapidly to be in communication with each other.[35] In this theory, as in the *ex nihilo* tradition, our universe did not arise from the remains of a previous universe. But in this theory the universe did not originate totally *ex nihilo* but from a Superspace of quantum fields and quantum laws.

Atheistic cosmologists are attracted to quantum fluctuation theory partly because it allows them to avoid the unique beginning associated with traditional theism. Rem Edwards suggests, however, that the theory is compatible with a revised process theism that includes both distinctive events in the initiation of universes and a continuing divine activity in each universe. God's everlasting creativity and sociality would be expressed both in Superspace and in innumerable finite universes. Edwards holds that the space and time of our universe are finite but were created within an infinite Superspace—not by chance but by God's selection among potential universes. In such a scheme God is always related to some universe but not always to our particular cosmic history.[36] Still, this is a highly speculative theory because other universes are in principle unobservable from our universe.

The simplest cosmological option is *a unique Big Bang,* a view which does not postulate unobservable cycles or unobservable universes. This option assumes a beginning in time and is closest to the *ex nihilo* tradition. Whitehead himself said that God's primordial nature transcends our cosmic epoch. In process thought the limitation of God's power over events within cosmic history arises not only from God's nature but also from the influence of past events on subsequent events. Moreover, in the course of cosmic history, events at higher levels of organization have greater self-determination, culminating in human freedom; and they have thereby a greater capacity to resist God's initial aims for them. These limitations arising from the past and from human freedom were not present in the early moments of the universe before even quarks existed. The pure potentialities in the primordial nature of God could have been more readily and rapidly realized in those dramatic early moments of the Big Bang than in subsequent history and would represent an essentially unilateral exercise of divine power, as the *ex nihilo* tradition affirms. However, to accept this option we would have to make a more extensive revision of Whitehead's thought than required by either cyclic or quantum fluctuation theories.

Scientific theories concerning the long-term future of the universe appear rather bleak. According to one scenario, the expansion of the universe will slow down and reverse itself, collapsing to a "heat death" that will end all forms of life. Astronomers have been searching for the "missing mass" (perhaps in neutrinos or interstellar dark matter) that might produce such a "closed universe." An alternative scenario expects the expansion to continue forever (an "open universe") leading to the "cold death" when temperatures are too low to support life. Recent evidence that the universe has been expanding more rapidly than previously assumed favors the second scenario. But before either of these cosmic catastrophes, our sun will have burnt itself out and life on our planet will be impossible. Long before then human folly may have ended human life by nuclear war or ecological disaster.

The Bible includes a wide variety of expectations of the future. The early prophets saw God's judgment in the disasters threatening the nation. But they believed that, if Israel returned to the covenant faith, it would enter a new era of peace, justice, and prosperity under a divinely appointed leader. Later, in the midst of oppression, the apocalyptic literature looked to the establishment of God's reign by the supernatural defeat of the oppressing powers. Within the New Testament, the reign was sometimes portrayed as growing slowly like a grain of mustard seed (Matthew 13), and in other passages as coming rapidly by a dramatic intervention (as in the Book of Revelation). Christ's return was sometimes imminently expected (as in Mark 13), while other authors held that it had already occurred spiritually in Christ's presence with his followers (the "realized eschatology" of John's Gospel).[37]

Liberals today, including process theologians, have usually favored a prophetic rather than an apocalyptic eschatology. But in reaction to the historical optimism of earlier decades, they acknowledge that the reign of God will not come by human effort alone. David Griffin points out that classical Christianity faced the problem of reconciling an omnipotent God and the continued existence of evil, and it sought an eschatological solution. He claims that process thought does not face this problem. It leads us to believe that God empowers us to resist evil now rather than to expect God's unilateral action in the future. It provides grounds for hope of God's victory over evil, but it offers no risk-free guarantee.[38]

4. Immortality and the Resurrection

As indicated in the previous chapter, most scholars maintain that the idea of an immortal soul temporarily inhabiting a mortal body, found in the early centuries of Christian history, was more indebted to Greek than to Hebrew thought. The Hebrew scriptures portrayed the human self as a unified bodily activity of thinking, willing, and acting. Paul defends the resurrection of the whole person by God's action, not the inherent immortality of a separate soul. Process thinkers have articulated two forms of immortality. Objective immortality, defended by Whitehead, refers to our effect on God and our participation in God's eternal life. Our lives are meaningful because they are preserved everlastingly in God's experience, in which evil is transmuted and the good is saved and woven into the harmony of the larger whole. God's goal is not the completed achievement of a static final realm but rather a continuing advance toward richer and more harmonious relationships.[39]

Other process writers defend subjective immortality, in which the human self continues as a center of experience in a radically different environment, amid continuing change rather than changeless eternity, with the potential for continued communion with God. John Cobb speculates that we might picture a future life as neither absorption in God nor the survival of separate individuals but as a new kind of community transcending individuality.[40] Marjorie Suchocki suggests that subjective and objective immortality can be combined, because God experiences each moment of our lives not merely externally as a completed event but also from within its subjectivity. In that case our subjective immediacy would be preserved in God as it never is in our interaction with other persons in the world.[41]

Finally, Christ's resurrection is a challenge to the idea of God's voluntary self-limitation presented earlier in this chapter. If Christ's death on the cross revealed God's suffering love, was this only a temporary strategy until God's true nature as omnipotent ruler was revealed in the resurrection? Religious art and popular piety have included images of both the agony of the crucifixion and the risen Christ ruling in glory. Martin Luther advocated both a "theology of the cross" and a "theology of glory." But theologians today who speak of God's voluntary self-limitation have the task of showing that the message of the resurrection does not cancel out the message of the cross.

Process theologians face a different challenge. Can process thought account for Easter? To be sure, scholars have questioned the historical accuracy of the resurrection stories. There are discrepancies among them, and Paul's letters, written earlier than the Gospels, never mention the empty tomb. But clearly the lives of the disciples were transformed in a dramatic way that changed the course of history. We could start by saying that the disciples became aware that in the midst of suffering God is present and new life is possible. They realized that God's love was not defeated by Christ's death. But we must also acknowledge their conviction that God had acted in a new way and that Christ had been taken up into the life of God and was a continuing influence on their lives. Marjorie Suchocki speaks of both confirmation and transformation: "The resurrection is the confirmation of that which Jesus revealed in his life and death, and it is the catalyst that transforms the disciples, releasing the power that led to the foundation of the church."[42] In process thought, God provides initial aims relevant to particular occasions, so very specific divine initiatives are possible, though always in cooperation with finite beings in the world. The events at Easter can be understood as such a new initiative.

I have suggested that process thought in its critique of divine omnipotence offers a distinctive rendition of four themes prominent in kenotic theology: the integrity of nature; the problem of evil, suffering, and human freedom; the Christian understanding of the cross; and feminist critiques of patriarchal models of God. I have tried to answer some possible criticisms of process theology concerning metaphysical necessity (rather than voluntary self-limitation) and the adequacy of God's power for redemptive action. I also discussed the beginning and end of the cosmos and the process interpretation of immortality and the resurrection. In all these contexts process thought offers a path between omnipotence and impotence by reconceptualizing divine power as empowerment rather than overpowering control.

6

Theology, Ethics, and the Environment

What are the implications of our view of God, nature, and human nature for the way we treat the environment? This chapter moves from theology to ethics and from pure science as a form of knowledge to applied science and technology as forms of action. After a brief historical introduction, I will ask how our understanding of the relation of God to nature and the relation of humanity to nonhuman nature affects our environmental attitudes and actions. The concluding section takes up issues of social justice and technology in a world of limited resources and economic globalization.

Historical Background

What roles have science and religion played in forming attitudes toward the environment?

1. Science and the Environment

During the 1970s we began to be aware of local environmental problems, especially the pollution of air, water, and land. Laws enacted by national and state governments have slowed the growth of many of the pollutants whose effects were immediately evident, and some steps were taken to preserve wildlife and natural environments. Since the 1980s scientists have been telling us about environmental impacts that are global, long-term, and cumulative. Topsoil is being rapidly eroded by intensive agriculture, overgrazing, and deforestation. Every year we are losing an area of tropical rainforest larger than the whole state of Pennsylvania. Each year we lose perhaps 50,000 endangered species, and with them we lose forever whole libraries of genetic information. Changes in the global climate caused by carbon dioxide from the burning of fossil fuels cannot be accurately predicted, but they are likely to be large enough to disrupt patterns of rainfall and agriculture. The world population is growing by 80 million each year, which is like adding the entire population of Mexico to the globe every year.[1] Industrial growth and the depletion of global resources by affluent nations raise additional questions of long-term sustainability that we have hardly begun to address. Scientists have studied these various environmental impacts and helped us to be more aware of them.

In relation to such scientific evidence, the main task of members of the religious community is to listen to scientists, to become better informed, and to help in spreading the word. But religious communities also have a responsibility to raise questions. They can ask scientists to indicate the assumptions and the uncertainties present in their interpretation of data. In the case of global warming, there is virtual unanimity among experts that increases in carbon dioxide and other greenhouse gases will lead to significant warming, though there is a range of estimates of probable temperature change (five to ten degrees Fahrenheit by the end of this century). It is now recognized that such changes are likely to trigger major alterations in weather patterns with drastic impacts on agriculture and coastal areas.[2] In other cases there may be greater disagreement among experts. Assessments of risks often depend on assumptions that should be made explicit since they may be influenced by a scientist's ethical or political convictions.

A scientist's recommendation of a particular policy of action is based in part on scientific estimates of the consequences of that policy. But policy recommendations inescapably involve value judgments in weighing the relative importance of diverse kinds of consequence. Furthermore, the benefits of a new technology or economic policy may accrue mainly to one group of people, while another group carries the burden of risks or indirect costs, so that issues of distributional justice are at stake. In addition, policy recommendations are the result of comparison with the alternatives that a person thinks are feasible and realistic—which introduces political and economic considerations. Policy decisions thus require ethical analysis and input from the social sciences and the wider culture as well as input from the natural sciences, even when the latter are as crucial as they are in decisions affecting the environment. In short, we need to rely heavily on the work of scientists without expecting them to have the last word on policy choices.[3]

2. An Indictment of Christianity

The discussion of the relation of theology to ecology in the 1970s was evoked by Lynn White's thesis that Christianity carries a heavy burden of responsibility for environmentally destructive attitudes in Western culture. White traced these attitudes back to two aspects of biblical thought. First, the Bible separated God from nature. Reacting to the nature religions of the surrounding cultures, the Israelites held that God was revealed primarily in history rather than in nature. Nature was desacralized, and God's transcendence was emphasized more than immanence. The second theme in White's influential essay was the separation of humanity from nonhuman nature in biblical thought. According to Genesis, human beings were given dominion over all other creatures. Humanity alone was said to be made "in the image of God" and set apart from all other creatures.[4]

When environmentalists repeated White's charges, some biblical scholars replied that human dominion is not absolute in Genesis because humanity is always under God; we are called to responsible stewardship. Moreover, many biblical passages celebrated the beauty of nature and its value to God, quite apart from its usefulness to us. Other scholars acknowledged the alienation of humanity from nature in classical Christianity but attributed it to the dualism of body and soul, which came into early Christianity from Hellenistic rather than from biblical sources. A different kind of reply to White came from historians, who said that economic forces were more important than religious beliefs in the growth of environmentally destructive practices. They pointed to the rise of capitalism, in which nature was viewed as a resource for human use and private profit, and the rise of technology and industry, through which human ability to harm nature increased dramatically. Other critics said that non-Christian cultures at various periods of history have perpetrated environmental damage just as severe as that in Christian cultures.

Feminist authors claimed that patriarchal views were a major contributor to environmental destruction. They noted the common assumptions underlying the domination of men over women and the domination of human beings over nature through technology. Men and technology were identified with the first term in each of the polarities of reason/emotion, mind/body, objectivity/subjectivity, and control/nurture. Women and nature were associated with the second term in each case. Feminists saw the oppression of women and the oppression of nature as rooted in a common set of hierarchical, dualistic, patriarchal assumptions. They proposed more holistic and ecological models of the relation of both God and humanity to nature.[5]

My own conclusion is that many factors entered into Western attitudes toward nature and that Lynn White oversimplified a complex historical phenomenon. But the two problems that he emphasized, the separation of God and nature and the separation of humanity and nature, were indeed characteristic of Medieval and subsequent Christian thought. Theology, preaching, liturgy, and ritual focused on the doctrine of personal redemption rather than the doctrine of creation. Redemption was usually seen as an escape from creation rather than the fulfillment of creation. In much of later Christian thought, including many conservative and evangelical authors in our own day, nature is the stage or backdrop for the drama of salvation, not an essential part of the drama. White's historical account may be questioned, but he was surely right that the environmental crisis is a call to critical theological reflection.

3. An Ecumenical Approach

An interesting analysis of the potential contribution of the Christian tradition to environmental policy was given by Max Oelschlaeger in *Caring for the Earth: An Ecumenical Approach*. He argues that fundamental environmental issues have not been addressed because short-term economic criteria have dominated policy choices. Citizens vote according to their individual economic interests. Politicians run on platforms of economic growth and lower taxes. Economists measure progress by the GNP, which omits environmental costs and discounts future costs and benefits. Corporations seek immediate profits, and they have enormous power over elected representatives through their campaign contributions. As a nation we are dedicated to a high-consumption lifestyle, and we assume that new technologies or technical fixes will overcome any problems created by industrial growth.[6]

Oelschlaeger's thesis is that the church is the only institution that can effectively challenge this dominance of short-term economic criteria in public policy. The church has been a strong voice in political life in the past, for example in the abolition of slavery, in women's suffrage, in the civil rights movement, and in opposition to the Vietnam War. Today it is one of the few institutions in which individualism can be challenged and the public good discussed. Oelschlaeger grants that many churches are focused exclusively on personal salvation or have been co-opted by the prevailing consumerism or restrict themselves to a narrow range of public issues. But he claims that the church has an enormous potential to influence environmental politics because it can ask basic questions about the goals of life. It can support nonmarket values, such as social justice, environmental preservation, and the welfare of future generations. He notes that the Catholic Church and all the major Protestant denominations have issued strong environmental statements.

Oelschlaeger says that creation stories in any culture are particularly important because they place individual life in a wider context of meaning. Creation stories are emotionally evocative and they support shared values and patterns of behavior. Ninety-five percent of Americans say they believe in God, and they could be a strong voice for the environment if they united around the common theme of "caring for creation." Oelschlaeger gives examples of environmental writings from across the theological spectrum: such conservatives as Francis Schaeffer and Calvin DeWitt; such moderates as Susan Bratton, James Nash, and the U.S. Catholic bishops; liberals including John Cobb, Jay McDaniel, Teilhard de Chardin, and Rosemary Radford Ruether; and radicals like Thomas Berry and Matthew Fox. His fifth category, which he calls "alternative creation stories," includes goddess feminism and Native American traditions. He says that instead of arguing about differing truth claims among these diverse theologies, we should take a pragmatic approach, seeking consensus at the level of political action. We should not get involved in debates with biblical literalists about whether to accept or reject evolution. Instead, we should seek common ground in "caring for creation" in order to save our endangered planet.

I agree with Oelschlaeger that we must cooperate ecumenically, drawing from our varied traditions in a common effort to promote the care of the earth. However, I disagree with his assertions that theological differences are unimportant and that science and religion are totally unrelated. He holds that neither science nor religion provides true statements about reality; they are both sociolinguistic cultural constructions that are useful in human life. Drawing from pragmatist and linguistic philosophers, he argues that science and religion are independent language systems that can only be judged by their usefulness. Science is "another among many language games that humans play" and it should not be accorded a privileged position.

By contrast, I would argue that in both science and religion we try to understand reality, but in neither do we find unchanging or complete certainty. Both science and religion make use of conceptual models that are partial representations of relationships that cannot be directly observed. Both involve assumptions that must be tested against the ongoing experience of a community of inquiry. Science and religion overlap at some points when they make statements about a common world. Religious beliefs may therefore need to be reformulated in the light of scientific understanding. In particular, our doctrines of creation and human nature must take evolution and ecology into account.

God and Nature

Let us look at the first issue raised by Lynn White, God's relation to nature. I will summarize four themes that support a Christian environmentalism.[7]

1. Stewardship and Celebration

Many recent theological writings, especially by conservative and evangelical authors, give prominence to the biblical injunction of stewardship. According to Deuteronomy, "The earth is the Lord's." The land belongs ultimately to the God who created it; we are only trustees or stewards, responsible for its welfare and accountable for our treatment of it. Several biblical passages call for humane treatment of domestic animals. The Sabbath is a day of rest for the earth and other living things as well as for people. Every seventh year the fields are to lie fallow; the land deserves respect, and it will cry out if mistreated (Lev. 25:1-5). In many rural churches today, Land Stewardship Sunday is celebrated in June, and the conservation of soil and other natural resources is encouraged. This stewardship concept can be extended to all natural resources and all forms of life.[8]

Stewardship is not centered on humanity alone, since it includes responsibility to God and concern for the welfare of other creatures. But unless it is coupled with other biblical themes, it can readily be distorted to assign a purely utilitarian value to nature. Taken alone, it seems to objectify nature and distance humans from it as a sphere for us to manage. But when taken with other themes, stewardship can contribute to an ethic of care and responsibility for the natural world.

Celebration goes beyond stewardship because it sees nature as valuable in itself. Genesis 1 ends with an affirmation of the goodness of the created order. The idea of creation is a great unifying framework, encompassing all forms of life. The covenant after the flood includes all creatures (Gen. 6:18-19). Many of the Psalms refer to the value of nature apart from its usefulness to us (e.g., Ps. 148: 9-10). Psalm 104 celebrates the rich diversity of nature and concludes: "O Lord, how manifold are thy works! In wisdom hast thou made them all; the earth is full of thy creatures" (Ps. 104:24). At the end of his dialogue with God, Job is overwhelmed by the majesty of natural phenomena, including strange creatures that are of no use to humanity (Job 40-41). Jesus spoke of God's care for the lilies of the field and the sparrows of the air, and several of his parables use images from the natural world. Among recent authors, James Nash has argued that God's love extends to include all creatures. We in turn respond by loving what God loves, and by caring for God's beloved creatures.[9]

Liturgies and prayers expressing gratitude for the created order are more common than they were twenty-five years ago. Some excellent new hymns have been written and appear in denominational hymnbooks. In addition to Thanksgiving harvest festivals, congregational services built around creation are sometimes offered at other times of the year, though they are obviously far outweighed by the number of services built around redemption or the historical events celebrated in the church year. Only rarely is celebration accompanied by repentance for our attitudes and actions that have been harmful to the natural world.

2. The Holy Spirit in Nature

The biblical idea of Spirit seems to me particularly helpful in thinking about God's relation to nature. In the opening verses of Genesis, "the Spirit of God was moving over the face of the waters." The Hebrew word for spirit, *ruach,* also means breath; God breathes the breath of life into the creation. Several of the psalms speak of the presence of the Spirit in nature. In Psalm 104, the Spirit is the agent of continuing creation in the present: "Thou dost cause the grass to grow for the cattle, and plants for man to cultivate. . . . When thou sendest forth thy Spirit, they are created." The same root is found in the word *inspiration;* the Spirit inspires the prophets and the worshipping community. Jesus received the Spirit at his baptism and according to Luke was full of the Holy Spirit as he started his ministry. The activity of the Spirit marked the birth of the church at Pentecost. Within the Bible, reference to the Spirit thus ties together God's work as Creator and as Redeemer. The Spirit is also free of the male imagery associated with the Father and the Son.[10]

Nonetheless, the early church tended to identify the work of the Spirit almost exclusively with redemption. As the doctrine of the Trinity was developed in the Western church, the Holy Spirit was subordinate to the Eternal Son and was said to come from the Son. In the Middle Ages the sacraments and the institutional church were taken to be the main channels for the operation of the Spirit. Protestantism saw the work of the Spirit in the life of individual believers.

The Spirit was said to witness within us to the truth of scripture or to bring us to conversion to Christ. Pentecostal and charismatic groups held that the work of the Spirit is manifest in prophecy, speaking in tongues, and other unusual powers. In all of these cases, the biblical understanding of God's indwelling presence in nature as the life-giving Spirit was ignored. Greater attention to the Spirit can help us find a better balance between transcendence and immanence in thinking about God's relation to nature today.

3. The Redemption of Nature

The prophetic vision of future harmony and wholeness, or *shalom,* includes the whole of creation and not humanity alone. Hosea says that human actions harm nature. "Therefore the land mourns, and all who dwell in it languish, and also the beasts of the field, and the birds of the air; and even the fish of the sea are taken away" (4:3). Hosea envisions God making a new covenant that includes all creatures: "And I will make for you a covenant on that day with the beasts of the field, the birds of the air, and the creeping things of the ground" (2:18). Paul writes that "the whole creation has been groaning in travail together until now," but he is confident that it will all take part in the final fulfillment (Rom. 8:22). The eschatological vision of the healing and renewal of creation looks to a future event, but it also casts light on the present and the goals of our own actions.[11]

Other biblical passages affirm that Christ as the Eternal Son had a role in creation as well as redemption. Paul writes that "all things were created through him and for him. He is before all things, and in him all things hold together" (Col. 1:16-17). In the early church, Irenaeus maintained that in Christ God had entered the world to transform the whole creation and bring it into the divine life. Drawing on the Eastern Orthodox tradition, Paulos Gregarios has developed the image of the Cosmic Christ and the inclusion of all of nature in the domain of redemption.[12] The Greek Orthodox Metropolitan John of Pergamon holds that as priests of creation we can offer not just the bread and wine but all of nature to God. We can lift the material world with us into the realm of salvation and eternal life. Both Christ and humanity, he says, are essential links between God and the world to bring the redemption of all creation.[13]

I see here an affirmation of the value of the natural world because it is included in the realm of redemption. On the other hand I see a danger in overemphasizing the idea that nature needs redemption. Some theologians have asserted that nature is fallen because of human sin. In particular, the idea that death and suffering entered nature because of human sin is surely incompatible with our understanding of evolutionary history, though we can acknowledge that sinful human actions have harmed other creatures whose lives are intimately bound with ours. We can act as priests of creation in celebrating it and holding it up to God, but we cannot claim to be the primary mediators between God and creation if we affirm God's presence and activity in the world.

4. The Sacred in Nature

A further step in asserting the value of nature is the belief that the sacred is present in and under it. Eastern Orthodoxy celebrates the goodness and beauty of creation and finds God's presence in it, holding that the infinite is manifest in the finite. Celtic Christianity, influenced by pre-Christian nature worship in Britain and Ireland, expresses a deep love of the natural world and a conviction that God is immanent in it. Several Anglican authors suggest that all of nature, and not just the bread, wine, and water of the sacraments, can be a vehicle of God's grace. These traditions have a strong sense of the community of life and they seek to heal the divisions within it.[14] According to Pierre Teilhard de Chardin, matter is permeated by creative power and by spirit, and all nature is sacred. In *The Divine Milieu* he acknowledges the presence of the divine throughout the created order as well as in human life.[15]

Some of the great Christian mystics have affirmed the presence of the sacred in nature. For them, the unity of all things is found not only in the depth of the individual soul but also in encounter with nature. Meister Eckhart, Hildegard of Bingen, and Julian of Norwich expressed a world-affirming rather than a world-denying mysticism. They held that in meditation and in a response of all-inclusive love we can realize the divinity within us and within nature. Matthew Fox has advocated a creation-centered spirituality that responds in awe and wonder to the cosmos as understood by modern science. He says that, by stressing original sin, classical Christianity failed to appreciate creation as "original blessing." He urges us to celebrate the sacredness of nature in song, dance, ritual, and art. Fox sees himself as remaining within the Christian tradition and reinterpreting it, though the person of Christ is not as central in his writings as in those discussed above.[16]

One can of course go even further and seek the sacred in nature, quite apart from Christianity. Many people have reported an experience of the holy in a natural setting. Nature poets such as William Wordsworth and Alfred Lord Tennyson and essayists such as Ralph Waldo Emerson and John Muir testify to a spiritual aspect of nature.

Aldo Leopold, Rachael Carson, Loren Eisley, and other scientists have spoken of their awe, humility, and gratitude in confronting the natural world. This more experiential dimension of encounter with nature can greatly enrich our lives and motivate our action, whether we interpret it within a theistic, a pantheistic, or a naturalistic framework.

Within a Christian context, the sacredness of nature is qualified by some of the other themes above. Transcendence is a spatial metaphor, but it need not be understood literally as referring to God's distance from the world in a way that excludes immanence. There is, to be sure, some tension between the sacramental sense of the sacredness of what is and the prophetic awareness of the imperfection of the present and the sacredness of what might be. There are dangers in a romanticism that neglects struggle and cruelty among creatures and sinfulness in human life. Some of the nature poets and mystics have lacked the prophetic recognition of the social structures of power and injustice that do violence to persons and to the natural world. I believe that these four themes (stewardship and celebration, the Holy Spirit, the redemption of nature, and the sacred in nature) must be taken together and combined with a concern for social justice, which I will consider later.

Humanity and Nature

We have been looking at God's relation to nature. Let us turn to the second issue, raised by Lynn White: the relationship of humanity to the rest of nature.

1. Human Nature: Beyond Dualism

Genesis states that we are made in the image of God. As we saw in chapter 3, the *imago Dei* has usually been interpreted as a human ability, such as rationality, spirituality, or moral agency. It has often been taken to set us apart totally from all other creatures and to justify our dominion over them. But other authors have suggested that the image refers to our relation to God and our capacity to reflect God's purposes—which include respect for all creatures. The story of Adam's fall cannot of course be taken literally in the light of evolutionary history, but it can be taken as a powerful symbolic expression of human sinfulness, where sin is understood as self-centeredness and estrangement from God and other people—and also from the world of nature.

In the Bible, as we noted in chapter 4, body, mind, and spirit are looked on as aspects of a single personal unity. The self is a unified bodily agent who thinks, feels, wills, and acts. The body is not considered the source of evil or something to be denigrated or escaped. Persons in their wholeness are the object of God's saving purposes. In the biblical view, selfhood is always social, for we are constituted by our relationships and the covenants we enter. We are always persons-in-community, not isolated individuals.

But under the influence of late Greek thought, the early church increasingly viewed a human being as a separate soul temporarily inhabiting a body. This dualism was continued in the modern period in René Descartes's distinction between mind and matter as radically different substances with no properties in common. An absolute line was drawn between humanity and all other creatures, for only humans were said to have souls or the capacity for rational thought. In the eighteenth and nineteenth centuries, many authors found such a dualism untenable and kept only one half of it, the material side. For them, human beings as well as the rest of nature were to be explained in materialistic and reductionistic terms.

Without reverting to dualism, we can today reject reductionistic materialism and acknowledge human beings as responsible persons. As in the biblical view, we can accept the holistic character of persons as integrated centers of thinking, feeling, willing, and acting. We can accept the social and bodily character of selfhood. Taking science into account, we can think of ourselves as many-leveled psychosomatic beings. We need distinctive concepts to understand activities at different levels. During evolutionary history, changes among life-forms were gradual and continuous, but they added up to dramatic differences in ability and behavior. Most biologists acknowledge the distinctiveness of human self-consciousness, language, and culture. Human beings are capable of intellectual and artistic creativity and personal relationships far beyond anything found among other creatures. We are indeed set apart from the rest of nature but not in the absolute way classical Christianity maintained.[17]

2. Kinship with All Creatures

Human kinship with other forms of life is stated or implied in a number of biblical passages. The story of Noah is myth rather than history, but in its own way it acknowledges the value of biodiversity. The Psalms refer to our companionship with other creatures. For St. Francis, a spiritual bond connects us with all creatures, while St. Benedict promoted agricultural and resource practices that treated nature with respect. In Celtic Christianity, other creatures are our companions in the fellowship of creation.

We can also learn from indigenous religious traditions that have had a strong sense of kinship among all creatures. Native Americans conceive of nature as an extended family, a community of beings with reciprocal responsibilities. All forms of life are members of a natural social order, whose harmony and balance should be maintained. Humans are linked to other creatures and dependent on them, as portrayed in tribal stories and acknowledged in tribal rituals. All creatures should be treated with respect because they too participate in a spiritual world whose power is experienced in dreams and visions. Native Americans also feel a strong identification with the land and with particular mountains and rivers that have been important in their history.[18] Recent studies claim that environmentalists have romanticized Native American life, which often failed to live up to such ideals (for example, large herds of buffalo were driven off cliffs and only a few of them were used for food and clothing).[19] Nevertheless, the Native American sense of kinship with nonhuman life stands in strong contrast to dominant American attitudes.

Many fields of science have traced the interdependence of diverse forms of life. The study of ecosystems shows the complex interconnections in the web of life. While some ecosystems are quite resilient, others are fragile and vulnerable to the repercussions of human actions. Diversity in the biosphere allows for both stability and adaptation to new conditions. Beyond the study of specific interactions among life-forms, ecology has led to a new understanding of our dependence on our environments. As we have seen in earlier chapters, evolutionary biology has also given us a new perception of our place in nature and has shown our kinship with other creatures. We are united in a common cosmic story that goes back to the early stars in which were formed the atoms in our brains and in all plants and animals. Life on earth is the story of our family tree of descent from common ancestors. The same genetic code is used in the DNA of all forms of life. Diverse species evolved together and influenced each other's evolutionary history.

Enlightened self-interest should lead us to consider the impact of our actions on other life-forms. But many scientists go further in criticism of a purely anthropocentric viewpoint. They are concerned for the wider web of life, and they value other creatures in themselves, not simply for their usefulness to us. Some of them, such as the biologist Ursula Goodenough, have given eloquent expression to their experience of unity with and participation in the world of nature.[20] They respond to the cosmos with a sense of awe and wonder and regard the earth as in some sense sacred. Such personal and reflective responses go beyond science itself, but they provide strong motivation for action to preserve the environment.

3. Process Theology

The process philosophy of Alfred North Whitehead and his followers is ecological in holding that every entity is constituted by its relationships. It is evolutionary in accepting a long history of continuous change in which no absolute lines can be drawn between successive forms of life. We have seen that in process thought every unified entity is considered to be a moment of experience. The character of that experience varies widely between an amoeba with rudimentary responsiveness, an animal with conscious purposes, and a self-conscious human being reflecting on future goals. Process philosophy offers an alternative to mind/body dualism, without adopting materialism on the one hand or idealism on the other. It holds that all integrated entities have an objective, external aspect and an experiential, internal aspect. Interiority or experience is present in lower forms, but only at higher levels of complexity does mind or consciousness emerge.[21]

According to process thought, all creatures have value to God and to each other, and all have intrinsic value as centers of experience. But creatures vary widely in their richness of experience and in their contribution to the experience of other beings, so they are not equally valuable. This view would lead us to work for the welfare of all forms of life, but it also suggests priorities when the needs of human and nonhuman life conflict. Process thought differs from a biocentric ethics, which says that we should choose whatever actions further the welfare of the ecosystem as a whole, regardless of the interests of individuals. It shares with advocates of animal rights a concern for the suffering of individual animals, but it extends that concern to all forms of life in varying degrees. A human being is more valuable than a mosquito to itself, to other beings, and to God. Because process thought holds that individuals are constituted by their relationships, process thought stands between the holism of biocentric ethics and the individualism of theories of animal rights.

Process theologians also have a distinctive answer to the question of God's relation to nature. Traditional theology emphasized divine transcendence and the gap between God and nature. At the opposite extreme, romanticism, pantheism, nature mysticism, and some of the New Age movements today have emphasized immanence, which usually leads to an impersonal God or identifies God with nature. According to process thought, God transcends nature but is also immanent in the temporal process, for God is present in the unfolding of every event. This implies that nature is not to be exploited, on the one hand, or worshiped, on the other, but is to be respected and appreciated, for it is the scene of God's continuing activity[22]

Justice, Technology, and the Environment

Environmental policies are inseparable from questions of social justice both within industrial nations and globally among nations. What contribution might the biblical tradition make to the interlocking problems of sustainability, environmental preservation, technological development, and economic globalization?

1. Sustainability, Consumption, and Population

We are related to nature not as isolated individuals but as members of social institutions that have far-reaching impacts on the environment. The environmental crisis raises questions about sustainability, patterns of consumption, and population growth.

1. A Long-Term View. Degraded land, eroded soil, and decimated fisheries and forests will take many decades to recover. We are living off biological capital, not biological income. Many of the impacts of our technologies will be felt by future generations. Radioactive wastes from today's nuclear power plants will endanger anyone exposed to them 10,000 years from now. The world of politics, however, takes a very short-term view. Political leaders find it difficult to look beyond the next election. The main concern of business and industry is this year's bottom line. Economic calculations give little weight to long-term consequences because a time discount is applied to future costs and benefits.

The biblical tradition, by contrast, takes a long-term view. Stewardship requires consideration of the future because God's purposes include the future. The Bible speaks of a covenant from generation to generation "to you and your descendants forever." The land, in particular, is to be held as a trust for future generations. This long time-perspective derives from a sense of history and ongoing family and social life, as well as accountability to a God who spans the generations. So it is not surprising that sustainability has been a major theme in statements of the World Council of Churches, several Protestant denominations, and the U.S. Conference of Catholic Bishops.[23] A long-term view is also common among scientists, especially those who are familiar with the long sweep of cosmic and evolutionary history. Ecologists study populations over many generations and are keenly aware that population growth puts increasing strains on ecosystems and jeopardizes the welfare of future generations.

2. *A Global Perspective.* Both the scientific and the religious communities at their best have advocated a global perspective. Science itself is international. Scientific meetings and journals ignore national boundaries. Scientists have a global viewpoint on environmental and resource problems. They recognize that impacts on the environment at one point have far-reaching repercussions at distant points. Chlorofluorocarbons released in repairing an air-conditioner in Boston will contribute to the depletion of ozone and the risk of skin cancer in Berlin or Bangkok. Scientists have insisted that an adequate response to global warming can be achieved only by international agreement on the reduction of greenhouse emissions. They have been aware of the destructiveness of nuclear war and have been prominent in the arms control and peace movements and in supporting the U.N. However, we must acknowledge that scientists are subject to the same nationalistic viewpoints as other citizens, and many applied scientists have been working directly or indirectly on military projects.

Our religious traditions have also held up a vision of world community, though they have too often succumbed themselves to intolerance and religious imperialism. The biblical writers affirm our common humanity and assert that we have been made "one people to dwell on the face of the earth." The religious communities of the U.S. have been active in working for peace and for support of the U.N. They have organized famine relief and lobbied for foreign aid and agricultural and technical assistance. Most religious groups have been urging a reduction in military expenditures and have criticized reliance on nuclear weapons. Religious leaders can join scientists in asserting that future threats to the nation's security are likely to be economic and environmental as well as military. The World Council of Churches has insisted that our response to these threats must be global and international rather than narrowly national.[24]

3. *Consumption and Visions of the Good Life.* Conservation policies in industrial nations would of course contribute substantially to a more just and sustainable world. Greater efficiency, waste recovery, and cleaner technologies can cut down on both pollution and resource use. But I believe we must go beyond efficiency and look at our patterns of consumption. By the age of twenty, the average American has already seen 350,000 television commercials. The mass media hold before us the images of a high-consumption lifestyle. Self-worth and

happiness are identified with consumer products. Our culture encourages us to try to fill all our psychological needs through consumption. Consumerism is addictive, and like all addictions it involves the denial of its consequences. Yet several studies have shown that there is very little correlation between happiness and income or wealth, whereas happiness does have a high correlation with marriage relationships, family life, work satisfaction, friendship, and community involvement.[25]

The Christian tradition offers a vision of the good life that is less resource consumptive than prevailing practices. It holds that, once basic needs are met, true fulfillment is found in spiritual growth, personal relationships, and community life. This path is life-affirming, not life-denying. Religious faith speaks to the crisis of meaning that underlies compulsive consumerism. We should seek a level of sufficiency that is neither ever-growing consumption nor joyless asceticism. A vision of positive possibilities and an alternative image of the good life are likely to be more effective than moral exhortation in helping people to turn in new directions. For most people in our nation, restraint in consumption is indeed compatible with personal fulfillment. We can try to recover the Puritan virtues of frugality and simplicity, both in individual lifestyles and in national policies.[26] For the Third World, of course, and for low-income families in industrial nations, levels of consumption must rise substantially if basic needs are to be met.

4. Population Growth. In addition to per capita consumption, the size of the population is an important factor in the depletion of natural resources. The average number of children per couple has been slowly falling in most of the Third World, but the total population is growing faster than ever because of the large number of young people entering childbearing years. The Program of Action adopted by the United Nations Population Conference in Cairo in 1994 gave major emphasis to the empowerment of women through access to education, health care, and political and economic equality. The document recognized that birth rates fall when women have more control over their lives. It also called for access to "safe, effective, affordable and acceptable methods of family planning of their choice." Moreover, it pointed to the importance of economic development both as a goal in itself and as a way of encouraging population stability.[27]

Many church groups were active participants among the nongovernmental organizations at Cairo. The Vatican stood virtually alone in opposing contraception, though it does not have the support of most Roman Catholics (who practice contraception in almost exactly the same proportion as non-Catholics). Conservative Protestants do not object to contraception, but they have been concerned that the U.N. would allow abortions as a means of controlling family size, and on those grounds they persuaded the Reagan and both Bush administrations to withhold support for U.N. population programs. Mainstream Protestant groups have tried to separate the questions of contraception and abortion. They have also insisted that family planning must be included in the wider context of socioeconomic development in the South and disproportionate consumption and pollution by the North. Most Protestant leaders hold that human sexuality serves not only the goal of procreation but also that of expressing love and unity in marriage, so contraception is an acceptable means of responsible family planning.[28]

2. Environmental Justice in Industrial Nations

The effects of environmental damage fall very unevenly on different groups in society. The urban poor are exposed to higher levels of air pollution, water pollution, noise, and lead poisoning than citizens with higher incomes; and they have little economic or political power to defend themselves from such risks. Environmental injustice is a product not only of economic differences but also of residential and social inequalities. For example, black children from middle-income families are three times as likely to have lead poisoning as children from white families of identical income. Sixty percent of all African Americans live in communities with toxic waste sites. Companies looking for a site for a new waste facility are likely to choose an already polluted area in which they expect to encounter little opposition. There is evidence of discrimination in government decisions as to which sites will be cleaned up first, which has led to legislation seeking to enforce equal environmental protection. Another example of unequal risks is the high exposure to pesticides among migrant farm workers, who are predominantly Hispanic.[29]

Questions of social justice also arise when environmental regulations seem to jeopardize the jobs of workers. Companies have often threatened to close plants if pollution standards were tightened. A few such plants, especially those with heavily polluting or inefficient technologies, have actually closed. But most plants stayed open and the costs of pollution control were passed on to consumers. Overall, technologies for controlling pollution and improving efficiency have added more jobs to the economy than were lost by environmental regulations. While the demands of justice and of environmental preservation do sometimes conflict, they often can be combined. The exploitation of nature and of workers are typically products of the same economic and political forces. In Appalachia, both the landscape and the miners suffered because of the power of coal companies in state legislatures.

The marketplace neglects indirect costs, whether borne by nature or by people. Labor unions and environmentalists have often been on opposite sides of local and national issues, but now we see them cooperating on occupational health and safety and in demanding greater accountability by corporations and government bureaucracies. A political strategy dedicated to both justice and the environment will require a broad alliance that includes labor, environmental groups, community organizations, urban and civil rights advocates, the women's movement—and the churches.[30]

The Bible expresses the conviction that God is on the side of the poor and works for the liberation of the oppressed. The conviction goes back to the time of Moses and the liberation of the Hebrew slaves from Egypt. The ancient prophets spoke of God's judgment on their nation for allowing the rich to exploit the poor. Jesus opened his ministry by quoting Isaiah: "The Spirit of the Lord is upon me, because he has anointed me to preach good news to the poor. He has sent me to proclaim release to the captives . . . to set at liberty those who are oppressed" (Luke 4:18).

The biblical tradition is idealistic in its affirmation of creative human potentialities. Through technology we can use our God-given intellectual capacities to promote human flourishing. But the biblical tradition is also realistic about the abuse of power. Individuals tend to seek power and institutions rationalize their own self-interest, whether in corporations, labor unions, governments, or religious institutions. Some people today are optimistic about technology, focusing on its potential benefits. Others are pessimistic, pointing to ways in which technology threatens human dignity and the environment. Between the optimists and the pessimists are the contextualists, who claim that technology is an ambiguous instrument of power whose consequences depend on human choices and social institutions. I suggest that the biblical view of human nature would lead us to side with the contextualists. It would lead us not to oppose technology but to seek to direct it toward the basic needs of all people. Advances in information technology and biotechnology will lead to novel possibilities we can hardly imagine today, but we must have the humility to acknowledge human fallibility and environmental constraints that can be modified but never ignored.

Environmentalists have often neglected social justice, while social reformers have often neglected the environment. The religious community can bring these values together in a distinctive way because it believes God cares about both nature and people. The National Council of Churches combined these concerns when it started its program on Eco-justice. The World Council of Churches at its sixth assembly in 1983 adopted the theme: "Justice, Peace, and the Integrity of Creation."

3. Global Justice

Inequalities between nations are far greater than those within nations. Consumption by industrial countries is responsible for a grossly disproportionate share of global pollution and resource use. On average, a U.S. citizen consumes as much of the world's resources as forty citizens of India. Clearly the whole world could not possibly live at the level of U.S. affluence. More grain is consumed by livestock in the U.S. and the former Soviet Union than by the entire human population of the Third World. Our dogs and cats are better fed than most of the children in Africa. Some 250,000 children die each week from malnutrition and the diseases associated with it, while the U.S. pays farmers to reduce production of grains and dairy products. We import $1 billion in agricultural products each year from Central America, where a quarter of the children are malnourished.[31]

In many developing nations the best land is used for nonfood or luxury food crops for export rather than staple crops for local consumption. Enough food is produced globally to meet everyone's dietary requirements, but the rich can outbid the poor in the global supermarket. Vast areas of forest in Brazil have been cleared for export timber or to produce beef for American fast-food restaurants. In most of the Third World, land is concentrated in the hands of a few wealthy landowners—except for a few countries in which land reform has been achieved either peacefully or by revolutionary governments. Third World countries make larger payments in interest on debts than they receive in new loans and investments, resulting in a net flow of $50 billion each year from South to North, paid for largely by the export of crops, timber, and natural resources.[32] Disparities between rich and poor countries are perpetuated by new technologies that require extensive expertise, capital, and infrastructure. Computers and communication systems are sources of social power, and access to them varies greatly both within nations and between nations (the so-called digital divide). Biomedical research is directed mainly to the diseases of affluent societies, while tropical diseases affecting far larger populations are neglected.

4. The Globalization Debate

The flow of capital, resources, and products across national boundaries has been growing at unprecedented rates, facilitated by new communication technologies, such as satellites and the Internet, which in turn make possible a more rapid international diffusion of other technologies. Globalization opens far-reaching new opportunities, but it also raises significant ethical issues because conflicting values are at stake. Protests at recent meetings of the World Trade Organization and the World Bank have polarized the debate. Let me ask how the Christian understanding of human nature might illuminate these issues, with the caveat that specific policy choices require difficult judgments about economic and political questions on which thoughtful people may disagree.

1. Environmental Impacts. The International Monetary Fund has made its loans to developing nations contingent on the promotion of exports above all other goals. This policy has encouraged rapid deforestation, mineral extraction, and the growth of crops for export without regard for local needs or environmental consequences. The governments receiving loans have also been under pressure to reduce their budgets for environmental agencies and health services. To be sure, the World Bank has included sustainability and environmental preservation among its development goals, but only a small fraction of its structural adjustment loans have included environmental impact assessments.[33] Both the IMF and the World Bank should be required to give more attention to environmental consequences and to work more closely with the U.N. Environmental Program. I believe that we should try to reform and improve these agencies, rather than to abolish them as some critics suggest.

2. Low Wages in Developing Nations. Some economists have argued that wages must remain low in developing nations in order to attract foreign investment as a necessary first step toward economic growth. They say that these nations must accept pain in the short run for the sake of gain in the long run. But this raises ethical issues if foreign investors are making substantial profits on their overseas investments. It also raises practical questions about political stability and democratic institutions when Third World people feel that they have no control over their own destiny. Even if wages are somewhat higher than they would be without foreign investments, they are likely to remain low if workers are denied the right to form unions. Under pressure from lending agencies, public funding for education has been reduced, which will slow acquisition of the skills needed for better-paying jobs.[34]

3. Political Accountability. Within each nation we have recognized that market prices seldom include the indirect social and environmental costs of production, so we have introduced legislation through political processes to supplement unregulated market forces. But on the global scene there are no comparable democratic processes. Moreover, globalization has increased the power of economic institutions and decreased the power of political ones. Transnational corporations and banks have more economic power than most national governments. The World Trade Organization operates in secret, behind closed doors, and it can overrule national environmental and safety standards by claiming that they restrict trade. The inclusion of a wider spectrum of participants in WTO deliberations would make it more representative and more accountable.[35]

4. Transnational Corporations. It is easy to demonize transnational corporations and blame them for all the adverse effects of globalization. These corporations can indeed contribute to rising standards of living and the spread of innovative technologies. Some companies have taken steps to improve working conditions overseas. The biblical view of human nature would lead us to encourage such creative initiatives, but also to recognize that voluntary measures are not enough in a highly competitive world. In the polarized confrontations with protesters at recent international meetings, both sides claimed they were defending the public interest and that the other side was defending "special interests." Both sides oversimplified complex issues and caricatured their opposition. Religious communities are not immune to biases, but they do have diverse memberships and at their best they are committed to a broad range of values. They have the potential to present a balanced view of the public good if they inform themselves about the consequences of alternative policies.

5. New Technologies. At the outset new technologies are often expensive and available only to the affluent. But with mass production and technological improvements, the costs fall and they become more widely available. This occurs through market forces alone, but public policies can promote the wider diffusion of low-cost technologies. The Internet was first developed for military and governmental purposes, and then it was expanded for the benefit of corporations. But more recently it has been used to empower individuals and groups, including dissidents in China and protest movements around the world. In developing nations, urban elites were the first beneficiaries of the Internet, but satellites and cheap cell phones open new possibilities for access even in rural areas. For example, a program of small loans for cell phones to 5,000 villages in Bangladesh is offering new personal and commercial opportunities in one of the world's most impoverished areas.[36]

6. *Strengthening Communities.* The global market treats people primarily as consumers, and the global media are a homogenizing influence undermining local cultures. The civil society includes a variety of voluntary organizations larger than the family and smaller than the nation or corporation. They can give a voice to those who feel powerless. We must do all we can to strengthen community relationships. Churches, synagogues, mosques, and temples can provide stability in a time of rapid change. They can provide a supportive community to individuals who feel alienated from the impersonal and distant institutions affecting their lives, and they can motivate people to act to further the values they hold. A religious worldview can provide a standpoint for critical appraisal of the cultural values accompanying globalization.

The photographs of the earth taken by astronauts on the moon showed us our amazing planet as a whole for the first time. Science can help us to understand our planet. Technology can help us to use its resources more efficiently. Religion can help us to share both resources and technologies more equitably. There is enough for every need but not for every greed. Our task in the new millennium is to move toward a more just and sustainable society in which human beings are treated humanely and the creatures of planet Earth are treated with respect.

Acknowledgments

Several of these chapters draw from presentations given initially at conferences and subsequently published in conference proceedings. The published articles have been edited here to avoid repetition and to ensure continuity. They are used with the permission of the original publishers.

Chapter 2 is taken with only minor modifications from "Five Models of God and Evolution" in *Evolutionary and Molecular Biology: Scientific Perspectives on Divine Action,* Robert John Russell, William R. Stoeger, S.J., and Francisco J. Ayala, eds. (Vatican: Vatican Observatory; Berkeley, Calif.: Center for Theology and the Natural Sciences, 1998).

Chapter 3 started as a presentation in 1999 to a workshop of the Center for Theology and the Natural Sciences in Berkeley, California, but it incorporates my reading and reflection on human evolution and genetics since then.

Chapter 4 is a revised version of "Neuroscience, Artificial Intelligence, and Human Nature: Theological and Philosophical Reflections" in *Neuroscience and the Person: Scientific Perspectives on Divine Action,* Robert John Russell, Nancey Murphy, Theo C. Meyering, and Michael A. Arbib, eds. (Vatican: Vatican Observatory; Berkeley, Calif.: Center for Theology and the Natural Sciences, 1999).

An earlier version of chapter 5 appeared as "God's Power: A Process View" in *The Work of Love: Creation as Kenosis,* John Polkinghorne, ed. (Grand Rapids, Mich.: Eerdmans; London: SPCK, 2001).

The first three sections of chapter 6 are from "The Church in an Environmental Age" in *Earth at Risk: An Environmental Dialogue between Science and Religion,* Donald B. Conroy and Rodney L. Peterson, eds. (Amherst, N.Y.: Humanities Books, 2000). The last section was presented at the State of the World Forum 2000 held in New York in parallel with the United Nations Millennium 2000 meeting of world leaders.

141

Notes

Chapter 1: Introduction

1. Ian G. Barbour, *When Science Meets Religion* (San Francisco: HarperSan-Franciso, 2000).

2. Ian G. Barbour, *Religion and Science: Historical and Contemporary Issues* (San Francisco: HarperSanFrancisco, 1997).

Chapter 2: God and Evolution

1. Michael Ruse, *Philosophy of Biology Today* (Albany: State University of New York Press, 1988), 6; also his *The Darwinian Paradigm* (New York: Routledge, 1989).

2. David P. Depew and Bruce H. Weber, *Darwinism Evolving: Systems Dynamics and the Genealogy of Natural Selection* (Cambridge: MIT Press, 1995), Part I.

3. Ibid., Part II.

4. Robert N. Brandon and Richard M. Burian, eds., *Genes, Organisms, Populations: Controversies over the Units of Selection* (Cambridge: MIT Press, 1984); Niles Eldredge and Stanley N. Salthe, "Hierarchy and Evolution," in *Oxford Surveys of Evolutionary Biology* (Oxford: Oxford University Press, 1985).

5. Stephen Jay Gould, "Darwinism and the Expansion of Evolutionary Theory," *Science* 216 (1982): 380–87; Stephen Jay Gould and Niles Eldredge, "Punctuated Equilibrium Comes of Age," *Nature* 366 (1993): 223–27.

6. Stephen Jay Gould and Richard C. Lewontin, "The Spandrels of San Marco and the Panglossian Paradigm: A Critique of the Adaptionist Programme," *Proc. of Royal Society of London B* 205 (1979): 581–98.

7. G. Ledyard Stebbins and Francisco J. Ayala, "Is a New Evolutionary Synthesis Necessary?" *Science* 213 (1981): 967–71. See also Ayala, "Darwin's Devolution: Design without Designer," in *Evolutionary and Molecular Biology: Scientific Perspectives on Divine Action*, Robert John Russell, William R. Stoeger, S.J., and Francisco J. Ayala, eds. (Vatican: Vatican Observatory; Berkeley, Calif.: Center for Theology and the Natural Sciences,1998).

8. John Campbell, "An Organizational Interpretation of Evolution," in *Evolution at the Crossroads: The New Biology and the New Philosophy of Science*, David P. Depew and Bruce H. Weber, eds. (Cambridge: MIT Press, 1985).

9. C. H. Waddington, *The Strategy of the Genes* (New York: Macmillan, 1957); Robert J. Richards, *Darwin and the Emergence of Evolutionary Theories of Mind and Behavior* (Chicago: University of Chicago Press, 1987), chap. 10.

10. Ernst Mayr, *The Growth of Biological Thought* (Cambridge: Harvard University Press, 1982); also *idem*, "How Biology Differs from the Physical Sciences," in *Evolution at the Crossroads*, Depew and Weber, eds.

11. Ilya Prigogine and Isabelle Stengers, *Order out of Chaos: Man's New Dialogue with Nature* (New York: Bantam Books, 1984).

12. Stuart Kauffman, *The Origins of Order: Self-Organization and Selection in Evolution* (New York: Oxford University Press, 1993); *idem*, *At Home in the Universe: The Search for Laws of Self-Organization and Complexity* (New York: Oxford University Press, 1995).

13. Jeffrey S. Wicken, *Evolution, Thermodynamics, and Information: Extending the Darwinian Program* (New York: Oxford University Press, 1987).

14. George Halder, Patrick Callaerts, and Walter Gehring, "Induction of Ectopic Eyes by Targeted Expression of the *Eyeless* Gene in *Drosophila,*" *Science* 267 (1995): 1788–92.

15. Mae-Won Ho and Peter T. Saunders, eds., *Beyond Neo-Darwinism* (New York: Harcourt Brace Jovanovich, 1984); Brian Goodwin and Peter T. Saunders, eds., *Theoretical Biology: Epigenetic and Evolutionary Order from Complex Systems* (Edinburgh: Edinburgh University Press, 1989); see also Robert Wesson, *Beyond Natural Selection* (Cambridge: MIT Press, 1991).

16. See Thomas J. Kuhn, *The Structure of Scientific Revolutions*, 2d ed. (Chicago: University of Chicago Press, 1970); Imre Lakatos, "Falsification and the Methodology of Scientific Research Programmes," in *Criticism and the Growth of Knowledge*, ed. Imre Lakatos and Alan Musgrave (Cambridge: Cambridge University Press, 1970).

17. Fred Hoyle and Chandra Wickramasinghe, *Evolution from Space* (London: Dent, 1981).

18. Stanley N. Salthe, *Evolving Hierarchical Systems* (New York: Columbia University Press, 1985).

19. Kauffman, *At Home in the Universe*, chap. 4.

20. Ian G. Barbour, *Religion in an Age of Science* (San Francisco: Harper & Row, 1990), 96–104.

21. James Gleick, *Chaos: Making a New Science* (New York: Penguin Books, 1987); John Holte, ed., *Chaos: The New Science* (Lanham, Md.: University Press of America, 1993).

22. Stephen H. Kellert, *In the Wake of Chaos: Unpredictable Order in Dynamical Systems* (Chicago: University of Chicago Press, 1993).

23. For analyses of reduction, see Ian G. Barbour, *Issues in Science and Religion* (Englewood Cliffs, N.J.: Prentice-Hall, 1966), 324–37; and *idem, Religion in an Age of Science,* 165–69; Francisco J. Ayala, "Reduction in Biology," in *Evolution at the Crossroads,* Depew and Weber, eds.; Arthur Peacocke, *God and the New Biology* (London: Dent, 1986), chaps. 1 and 2.

24. Ian G. Barbour, *Religion and Science: Historical and Contemporary Issues* (San Francisco: HarperSanFrancisco, 1997), 230–37.

25. On top-down causation, see Donald Campbell, "'Downward Causation' in Hierarchically Organized Biological Systems," in *Studies in the Philosophy of Biol-*

ogy: *Reductionism and Related Problems,* Francisco J. Ayala and Theodosius Dobzhansky, eds. (Berkeley and Los Angeles: University of California Press, 1974); Michael Polanyi, "Life's Irreducible Structures," *Science* 160 (1968): 1308–12; Elisabeth Vrba, "Patterns in the Fossil Record and Evolutionary Processes," in *Beyond Neo-Darwinism,* Ho and Saunders, eds.

26. James Gleick, address at 1990 Nobel Conference, Gustavus Adolphus College, quoted in Steven Weinberg, *Dreams of a Final Theory* (New York: Pantheon Books, 1992), 61.

27. Charles R. Rosenberg and Terrence J. Sejnowski, "Parallel Networks That Learn to Pronounce English Text," *Complex Systems* 1 (1987): 145–68.

28. Bruce H. Weber and Terrence W. Deacon, "Thermodynamic Cycles, Developmental Systems, and Emergence," *Cybernetics and Human Knowing* 7, no. 1 (2000): 21–43.

29. Jeremy Campbell, *Grammatical Man: Information, Entropy, Language, and Life* (New York: Simon & Schuster, 1982).

30. Susan Oyama, *The Ontogeny of Information: Developmental Systems and Evolution* (Cambridge: Cambridge University Press, 1985).

31. Humberto R. Maturana and Francisco J. Varela, *The Tree of Knowledge: The Biological Roots of Human Understanding* (Boston: Science Library, 1987); Francisco J. Varela, Evan Thompson, and Eleanor Rosch, *The Embodied Mind: Cognitive Science and Human Experience* (Cambridge: MIT Press, 1991).

32. Ian G. Barbour, *Myths, Models, and Paradigms: A Comparative Study in Science and Religion* (New York: Harper & Row, 1974).

33. Barbour, *Religion and Science,* chap. 4.

34. Paul Davies, *The Cosmic Blueprint: New Discoveries in Nature's Creative Ability to Order the Universe* (New York: Simon & Schuster, 1988); *idem, The Mind of God: The Scientific Basis for a Rational World* (New York: Simon & Schuster, 1992).

35. Austin Farrer, *Faith and Speculation* (London: Adam & Charles Black, 1967), chaps. 4 and 10; William R. Stoeger, "Describing God's Action in the World in the Light of Scientific Knowledge of Reality," in *Chaos and Complexity: Scientific Perspectives on Divine Action,* Robert John Russell, Nancey Murphy, and Arthur Peacocke, eds. (Vatican: Vatican Observatory; Berkeley, Calif.: Center for Theology and the Natural Sciences, 1995).

36. William G. Pollard, *Chance and Providence* (New York: Charles Scribner's Sons, 1958); Donald M. MacKay, *Science, Chance, and Providence* (Oxford: Oxford University Press, 1978).

37. Nancey Murphy, "Divine Action in the Natural Order: Buridan's Ass and Schrödinger's Cat," in *Chaos and Complexity,* Russell et al., eds; Nancey Murphy and George F. R. Ellis, *On the Moral Nature of the Universe: Theology, Cosmology, and Ethics* (Minneapolis: Fortress Press, 1996).

38. Thomas F. Tracy, "Particular Providence and the God of the Gaps," and George F. R. Ellis, "Ordinary and Extraordinary Divine Action: The Nexus of Interaction," in *Chaos and Complexity,* Russell et al., eds.; Robert John Russell, "Special Providence and Genetic Mutation: A New Defense of Theistic Evolution" in *Evolution and Molecular Biology,* Russell et al., eds.

39. Arthur Peacocke, *Theology for a Scientific Age: Being and Becoming—Natural, Human, and Divine,* enlarged edition (Minneapolis: Fortress Press, 1993), chap. 3; *idem,* "God's Interaction with the World" in *Chaos and Complexity,* Russell et al.,

eds.; Peacocke, "Welcoming the 'Disguised Friend': A Positive Theological Appraisal of Biological Evolution" in *Evolutionary and Molecular Biology,* Russell et al., eds.

40. Peacocke, *Theology for a Scientific Age,* 217.

41. Grace Jentzen, *God's World, God's Body* (Philadelphia: Westminster Press, 1984); Sallie McFague, *The Body of God: An Ecological Theology* (Minneapolis: Fortress Press, 1993).

42. Arthur Peacocke, *Creation and the World of Science* (Oxford: Clarendon Press, 1979), chap. 3; *idem, Theology for a Scientific Age,* chap. 9.

43. Ibid.

44. John Polkinghorne, *Reason and Reality* (Philadelphia: Trinity Press International, 1991), chap. 3; *idem,* "The Metaphysics of Divine Action," in *Chaos and Complexity,* R. J. Russell ct al., eds; *idem, The Faith of a Physicist* (Princeton: Princeton University Press, 1994), 77–78.

45. John Puddefoot, "Information Theory, Biology, and Christology," in *Religion and Science: History, Method, Dialogue,* W. Mark Richardson and Wesley J. Wildman, eds. (New York: Routledge, 1996).

46. Alfred North Whitehead, *Science and the Modern World* (New York: Macmillan, 1925); *idem, Process and Reality* (New York: Macmillan,1929). See Barbour, *Religion and Science,* chap. 11.

47. Charles Hartshorne, *Reality as Social Process* (Glencoe, Ill.: Free Press, 1953).

48. James Hutchingson, "Organization and Process: Systems Philosophy and Whiteheadian Metaphysics," *Zygon* 11 (1981): 226–41.

49. Charles Birch, *A Purpose for Everything* (Mystic, Conn.: Twenty-Third, 1990); Charles Birch and John B. Cobb Jr., *The Liberation of Life: From the Cell to the Community* (Cambridge: Cambridge University Press, 1981).

50. Donald R. Griffin, *Animal Minds: Beyond Cognition to Consciousness* (Chicago: University of Chicago Press, 2001); Birch and Cobb, *The Liberation of Life.*

51. C. H. Waddington, "The Process of Evolution and Notes on the Evolution of Mind," in *Mind in Nature: Essays on the Interface of Science and Philosophy,* ed., John B. Cobb Jr. and David Ray Griffin (Washington D.C.: University Press of America, 1977).

52. John B. Cobb Jr. and David Ray Griffin, *Process Theology: An Introduction* (Philadelphia: Westminster Press, 1976).

53. G. W. H. Lampe, *God as Spirit* (Oxford: Clarendon Press, 1977); Alisdair Heron, *The Holy Spirit* (Philadelphia: Westminster Press, 1983).

54. Barbour, *Religion in an Age of Science,* 235–38.

Chapter 3: Evolution, Genetics, and Human Nature

1. A good survey of the fossil record of human evolution is given in Ian Tattersall, *The Human Odyssey: Four Million Years of Human Evolution* (New York: Prentice Hall, 1993). See also his *The Fossil Trail: How We Know What We Think We Know about Human Evolution* (New York: Oxford University Press, 1995).

2. Edward O. Wilson, *Sociobiology: The New Synthesis* (Cambridge: Harvard University Press, 1976).

3. Edward O. Wilson, *On Human Nature* (Cambridge: Harvard University Press, 1978), 176.

4. Richard Dawkins, *The Selfish Gene* (Oxford: Oxford University Press, 1977).

5. Robert Wright, "Our Cheating Hearts," *Time* 144 (August 15, 1994): 45–52. See also his *The Moral Animal: Evolutionary Psychology and Everyday Life* (New York: Pantheon Books, 1994).

6. Michael Ruse, *Taking Darwin Seriously* (Oxford: Basil Blackwell, 1986), 253.

7. Elliott Sober and David Sloan Wilson, *Unto Others: The Evolution and Psychology of Unselfish Behavior* (Cambridge: Harvard University Press, 1998).

8. Holmes Rolston III, *Genes, Genesis, and God: Values and Their Origins in Natural and Human History* (Cambridge: Cambridge University Press, 1999).

9. Jane Goodall, *The Chimpanzees of Gombe* (Cambridge: Harvard University Press, 1986).

10. Franz de Waal, *Good Natured: The Origins of Right and Wrong in Humans and Other Animals* (Cambridge: Harvard University Press, 1996).

11. R. A. Gardner and P. T. Gardner, "Teaching Sign Language to Chimpanzees," *Science* 165 (1969): 614–72.

12. E. Sue Savage-Rumbaugh, *Kanzi: The Ape at the Brink of the Human Mind* (New York: Wiley, 1994).

13. Terrence W. Deacon, *The Symbolic Species: The Co-evolution of Language and Brain* (New York: Norton, 1997), 340.

14. Merlin Donald, *The Origin of the Modern Mind: Three Stages in the Evolution of Culture and Cognition* (Cambridge: Harvard University Press, 1991), 382. See also his *A Mind So Rare: The Evolution of Human Consciousness* (New York: Norton, 2001).

15. Steven J. Mithen, *The Prehistory of Mind: The Cognitive Origins of Art and Science* (London: Thames and Hudson, 1996).

16. Ian Tattersall, *Becoming Human: Evolution and Human Uniqueness* (New York: Harcourt Brace, 1998).

17. Eugene G. d'Aquili, "The Myth-Ritual Complex: A Biogenetic Structural Analysis," *Zygon* 18 (1983): 247–69.

18. Victor Turner, "Body, Brain and Culture," *Zygon* 18 (1983): 221–45.

19. Roger Schmidt, *Exploring Religion* (Belmont, Calif.: Wadsworth Publishing, 1980), chap. 8.

20. Mircea Eliade, *The Sacred and the Profane* (New York: Harcourt, Brace & World, 1959), chap. 2.

21. Claude Levi-Strauss, *Structural Anthropology,* trans. C. Jacobsen and B. G. Schoepf (New York: Basic Books, 1963).

22. Eugene G. d'Aquili and Andrew B. Newberg, *The Mystical Mind: Probing the Biology of Religious Experience* (Minneapolis: Fortress Press, 1999); and *idem, Why God Won't Go Away* (New York: Ballantine, 2001).

23. Karl Jaspers, *The Origin and Goal of History* (New Haven: Yale University Press, 1953).

24. See Norman W. Porteous, "Image of God," in *Interpreters' Dictionary of the Bible* (Nashville: Abingdon, 1962), 2: 682–85.

25. Matthew Fox, *Original Blessing* (Santa Fe: Bear, 1983).

26. Paul Tillich, *The Shaking of the Foundations* (New York: Charles Scribner's Sons, 1948), 153–63, and *idem, Systematic Theology,* 3 vols. (Chicago: University of Chicago Press, 1951–63), 2: 44–78.

27. Pius XII, *Humani Generis* (1950); Raymond J. Nogar in *New Catholic Encyclopedia* (New York: McGraw-Hill, 1967–89), 5:682–95.

28. Reinhold Niebuhr, *The Nature and Destiny of Man* (New York: Charles Scribner's Sons, 1943), 1:173–77.

29. Reinhold Niebuhr, *The Children of Light and the Children of Darkness* (New York: Charles Scribner's Sons, 1944), xi.

30. Philip Hefner, *The Human Factor: Evolution, Culture, and Religion* (Minneapolis: Fortress Press, 1993), chap. 8.

31. Patricia A. Williams, *Doing without Adam and Eve: Sociobiology and Original Sin* (Minneapolis: Fortress Press, 2001).

32. Albert C. Outler, *Psychotherapy and the Christian Message* (New York: Harper & Brothers, 1954); Don S. Browning, *Religious Thought and the Modern Psychologies* (Minneapolis: Fortress Press, 1987).

33. John McIntyre, *The Shape of Christology* (Philadelphia: Westminster Press, 1966).

34. Donald Macpherson Baillie, *God Was in Christ* (New York: Charles Scribner's Sons, 1948).

35. Tillich, *Systematic Theology*, 2: 165–80.

36. Robert S. Franks, *The Work of Christ* (London and New York: Nelson, 1962).

37. G. W. H. Lampe, *God as Spirit* (Oxford: Clarendon Press, 1977).

38. Roger S. Haight, *Jesus Symbol of God* (Maryknoll, N.Y.: Orbis, 1999), 456. See also Paul W. Newman, *A Spirit Christology* (Lantham, Md.: University Press of America, 1987).

39. Steven J. Dick, ed., *Many Worlds: The New Universe, Extraterrestrial Life, and the Theological Implications* (Philadelphia: Templeton Foundation Press, 2000); Paul Davies, *Are We Alone?* (London: Penguin Books, 1995).

40. Stephen G. Post, *The Theory of Agape: On the Meaning of Christian Love* (Lewisburg, Pa.: Bucknell University Press, 1990); and *idem*, *Spheres of Love: Toward a New Ethic of the Family* (Dallas: S.M.U. Press, 1994).

41. Stephen J. Pope, *The Evolution of Altruism and the Ordering of Love* (Washington, D.C.: Georgetown University Press, 1994).

42. Philip Paul Hallie, *Lest Innocent Blood Be Shed: The Story of the Village of Le Chambon, and How Goodness Happened There* (New York: Harper & Row, 1979).

43. Joanne Carlson Brown and Carole R. Bohn, eds., *Christianity, Patriarchy, and Abuse: A Feminist Critique* (New York: Pilgrim Press, 1989).

44. James Watson, quoted in L. Jaroff, "The Gene Hunt," *Time* 133 (March 20, 1989): 67.

45. Walter Gilbert, "A Vision of the Grail," in *The Code of Codes: Scientific and Social Issues in The Human Genome Project*, Daniel J. Kevles and Leroy Hood, eds. (Cambridge: Harvard University Press, 1992), 96.

46. R. David Cole, "The Genome and the Human Genome Project" in *Genetics: Issues of Social Justice*, Ted Peters, ed. (Cleveland: Pilgrim Press, 1998).

47. Ted Peters, *For the Love of Children: Genetic Technology and the Family* (Louisville: Westminster John Knox, 1996).

48. J. Michael Bailey and Richard Pillard, "A Genetic Study of Male Sexual Orientation," *Archives of General Psychiatry* 48 (1991): 1089–96. See also Dean Hammer with Peter Copeland, *The Science of Desire* (New York: Simon & Schuster, 1994).

49. Troy Duster, "Persistence and Continuity in Human Genetics and Social Stratification," in *Genetics: Issues of Social Justice,* ed. Ted Peters.

50. See chapters by Ian Wilmot in *Engineering Genesis: The Ethics of Genetic Engineering in Non-Human Species,* Donald Bruce and Ann Bruce, eds., (London: Earthscan Publications, 1998).

51. Ronald Cole-Turner, ed., *Human Cloning: Religious Responses* (Louisville: Westminster John Knox, 1997); Ronald Cole-Turner, ed., *Beyond Cloning: Religion and the Remaking of Humanity* (Harrisburg, Pa.: Trinity Press International, 2001).

52. *Ethical Issues in Human Stem Cell Research,* vol. 3: *Religious Perspectives* (Rockville, Md.: National Bioethics Advisory Commission, 2000).

53. Joannie Fischer on *U.S. News and World Report* website, December 3, 2001.

54. Richard Lacayo, "How Bush Got There," *Time* 158 (August 20, 2001): 39–44.

55. See Suzanne Holland, Karen Lebacqz, and Laurie Zoloth, eds., *The Human Embryonic Stem Cell Debate: Science, Ethics and Public Policy* (Cambridge: MIT Press, 2001).

56. James Patterson, *Genetic Turning Points: The Ethics of Human Intervention* (Grand Rapids, Mich.: Eerdmans, 2001); Daniel C. Maguire, *Sacred Choices: The Right to Contraception and Abortion in Ten World Religions* (Minneapolis: Fortress Press, 2001).

57. James B. Nelson, *Human Medicine: Ethical Perspectives on New Medical Issues* (Minneapolis: Augsburg, 1973), chap. 1; James B. Nelson, *Body Theology* (Louisville: Westminster John Knox, 1992), chap. 10; Thomas A. Shannon and Allan B. Walter, "Reflections on the Moral Status of the Pre-Embryo," *Theological Studies* 51 (1990): 603–26; Lisa Sowle Cahill, "The Embryo and the Fetus: New Moral Contexts," *Theological Studies* 54 (1993): 124–42.

58. Mark S. Frankel and Audrey R. Chapman, *Human Inheritable Genetic Modification: Assessing Scientific, Ethical, Religious, and Policy Issues* (Washington, D.C.: American Association for the Advancement of Science, 2000).

59. Roger Lincoln Shinn, *The New Genetics: Challenges to Faith, Science, and Politics* (Wakefield, R.I.: Morgan Bell, 1996), chap. 5.

60. Lee M. Silver, *Remaking Eden: Cloning and Beyond in a Brave New World* (New York: Avon Books, 1997), 9, 11.

61. Ian G. Barbour, *Ethics in an Age of Technology,* Gifford Lectures, vol. 2 (San Francisco: HarperSanFrancisco, 1993), chap. 1.

62. Audrey R. Chapman, *Unprecedented Choices: Religious Ethics at the Frontiers of Genetic Science* (Minneapolis: Fortress Press, 1999), chap. 4.

63. Jeremy Rifkin, *Algeny* (New York: Penguin, 1984).

64. Ronald Cole-Turner, *The New Genesis: Theology and the Genetic Revolution* (Louisville: Westminster John Knox, 1993).

Chapter 4: Neuroscience, Artificial Intelligence, and Human Nature

1. Humberto R. Maturana and Francisco J. Varela, *The Tree of Knowledge: The Biological Roots of Human Understanding* (Boston: Science Library, 1987).

2. Michael A. Arbib, *The Metaphorical Brain 2: Neural Networks and Beyond* (New York: John Wiley, 1989), chap. 2.

3. Peter R. Kramer, *Listening to Prozac* (New York: Viking Penguin, 1993).

4. Oliver W. Sacks, *The Man Who Mistook His Wife for a Hat* (New York: HarperCollins, 1985).

5. Charles Darwin, *The Expression of the Emotions in Man and Animals* (Chicago: University of Chicago Press, 1965, orig. 1872); Carroll Izard, *Human Emotions* (New York: Plenum, 1977); John Tooby and Leda Cosmides, "The Past Explains the Present: Emotional Adaptations and the Structure of Ancestral Environments," *Ethology and Sociobiology* 11 (1990): 375–424.

6. William James, *The Principles of Psychology* (Cambridge: Harvard University Press, 1983, orig. 1890); R. W. Levenson, P. Ekman, and W. V. Friesen, "Voluntary Facial Action Generates Emotion-Specific Autonomic Nervous System Activity," *Psychophysiology* 27 (1990): 363–84.

7. Magda Arnold, *Emotion and Personality*, 2 vols. (New York: Columbia University Press, 1960); Richard Lazarus, "Progress on a Cognitive-Motivational-Relational Theory of Emotion," *American Psychologist* 46 (1991): 819–34.

8. James Averill, "The Social Construction of Emotion: With Special Reference to Love," in *The Social Construction of the Person*, K. J. Gergen and K. E. Davis, eds. (New York: Springer-Verlag, 1985); Rom Harré, ed., *The Social Construction of Emotions* (Oxford: Basil Blackwell, 1986).

9. Joseph E. LeDoux, *The Emotional Brain: The Mysterious Underpinnings of Emotional Life* (New York: Simon & Schuster, 1996).

10. Antonio R. Damasio, *Descartes' Error: Emotion, Reason, and the Human Brain* (New York: Putnam, 1994), 252.

11. Leslie A. Brothers, *Friday's Footprint: How Society Shapes the Human Mind* (New York: Oxford University Press, 1997), 146.

12. Sacks, *The Man Who Mistook His Wife for a Hat*, 22–41.

13. Ian G. Barbour, *Myths, Models, and Paradigms: A Comparative Study in Science and Religion* (New York: Harper & Row, 1974).

14. Paul MacLean, *The Triune Brain in Evolution* (New York: Plenum, 1990).

15. James B. Ashbrook and Carol Rausch Albright, *The Humanizing Brain: Where Religion and Neuroscience Meet* (Cleveland: Pilgrim Press, 1997).

16. Benjamin Libet, "Unconscious Cerebral Initiative and the Role of Conscious Will in Voluntary Action," *Behavioral and Brain Sciences* 8 (1985): 529–66.

17. Daniel C. Dennett, *Consciousness Explained* (Boston: Little, Brown, 1991), 141–44.

18. Donald R. Griffin, *Animal Minds* (Chicago: University of Chicago Press, 1992).

19. Terrence W. Deacon, *The Symbolic Species: The Coevolution of Language and the Brain* (New York: Norton, 1997).

20. Jerry A. Fodor, *The Modularity of Mind* (Cambridge: Harvard University Press, 1983).

21. Marvin Minsky, *The Society of Mind* (New York: Simon & Schuster, 1985).

22. Arbib, *The Metaphorical Brain 2*.

23. William Calvin, *The Cerebral Symphony* (New York: Bantam, 1989); *idem, The Cerebral Code* (Cambridge: MIT Press, 1996).

24. Dennett, *Consciousness Explained.*

25. Michael Gazzaniga, "Brain Modularity: Towards a Philosophy of Consciousness," in *Consciousness in Contemporary Science*, A. J. Marcel and E. Besiach, eds. (Oxford: Oxford University Press, 1988); see also *idem, Mind Matters: How Mind and Brain Interact to Create our Conscious Lives* (Boston: Houghton Mifflin, 1988).

26. Robert Ornstein, *Multimind* (Boston: Houghton Mifflin, 1986).

27. John Eccles, *Evolution of the Brain: Creation of the Self* (London: Routledge, 1989).

28. John Teske, "The Spiritual Limits of Neuropsychological Life," *Zygon* 31 (1995): 209–34.

29. Joel B. Green, "'Bodies—That Is, Human Lives': A Re-examination of Human Nature in the Bible," in *Whatever Happened to the Soul: Scientific and Theological Portraits of Human Nature,* Warren S. Brown, Nancey Murphy, and H. Newton Malony, eds. (Minneapolis: Fortress Press, 1998), chap. 7, 158.

30. Oscar Cullmann, *Immortality of the Soul or Resurrection of the Dead?* (New York: Macmillan, 1958), 30.

31. Lynn de Silva, *The Problem of Self in Buddhism and Christianity* (London: Macmillan, 1979), 75.

32. Norman W. Porteous, "Soul," in *The Interpreter's Dictionary of the Bible* (Nashville: Abingdon, 1962), 4: 428.

33. For example, Brevard Childs, *Biblical Theology of the Old and New Testaments* (Minneapolis: Fortress Press, 1993), chap. 7.

34. E. C. Blackman, "Mind," in *A Theological Word Book of the Bible,* Alan Richardson, ed. (New York: Macmillan, 1950), 145.

35. Walter Eichrodt, *Man in the Old Testament* (London: SCM Press, 1951); Frederick C. Grant, *An Introduction to New Testament Thought* (Nashville: Abingdon, 1950), 160–70.

36. David Kelsey, "Human Being," in *Christian Theology,* 2d ed., Peter Hodgson and Robert King, eds. (Philadelphia: Fortress Press, 1985).

37. James Keenan, *Goodness and Rightness in St. Thomas Aquinas's* Summa Theologiae (Washington, D.C.: Georgetown University Press, 1992).

38. See Ian G. Barbour, *Religion and Science: Historical and Contemporary Issues* (San Francisco: HarperSanFrancisco, 1997), chap. 1.

39. For example, Rosemary Radford Ruether, *Sexism and God-Talk: Toward a Feminist Theology* (Boston: Beacon Press, 1983).

40. H. Richard Niebuhr, *The Responsible Self* (New York: Harper, 1963), 73.

41. Alasdair MacIntyre, *After Virtue: A Study of Moral Theory,* 2d ed. (Notre Dame, Ind.: University of Notre Dame Press, 1984), chap. 15.

42. James B. Wiggins, ed., *Religion as Story* (New York: Harper & Row, 1975); Michael Goldberg, *Theology as Narrative: A Critical Introduction* (Nashville: Abingdon, 1982).

43. Keith Ward, *Defending the Soul* (London: Hodder and Stoughton, 1992).

44. Malcolm A. Jeeves, *Human Nature at the Millennium* (Grand Rapids, Mich.: Baker, 1997); idem, *Mind Fields: Reflections on the Science of Mind and Brain* (Grand Rapids, Mich.: Baker 1993). See also Donald M. MacKay, *Behind the Eye* (Oxford: Basil Blackwell, 1991).

45. Allan Newell and Herbert Simon, "Computer Science as Empirical Enquiry: Symbols and Search," originally published in 1976, reprinted in *Philosophy of Artificial Intelligence,* Margaret Boden, ed. (Oxford: Oxford University Press, 1990).

46. Hubert Dreyfus and Stuart Dreyfus, *What Computers Still Can't Do,* 3d ed. (Cambridge: MIT Press, 1993).

47. Terry Winograd and Fernando Flores, *Understanding Computers and Cognition: A New Foundation for Design* (Norwood, N.J.: Ablex Publishing, 1986).

48. David E. Rumelhart and James L. McClelland, eds., *Parallel Distributed Processing*, 2 vols. (Cambridge: MIT Press, 1986).

49. Stan Franklin, *Artificial Minds* (Cambridge: MIT Press, 1995), chap. 12.

50. Rodney A. Brooks and Luc Steels, eds., *The Artificial Life Route to Artificial Intelligence: Building Embodied, Situated Agents* (Hillsdale, Mich.: Laurence Erlbaum, 1995). See also Andy Clark, *Being There: Putting Brain, Body, and World Together Again* (Cambridge: MIT Press, 1997).

51. Anne Foerst, "COG, a Humanoid Robot, and the Question of *Imago Dei,*" *Zygon* 33 (1998): 91–111.

52. Roger Schank, "Natural Language, Philosophy, and Artificial Intelligence," in *Philosophical Perspectives on Artificial Intelligence*, M. Ringle, ed. (Brighton, England: Harvester Press, 1979), 222.

53. Aaron Sloman, "Motives, Mechanisms, and Emotions," in *Philosophy of Artificial Intelligence*, Boden, ed.; see also Keith Oatley, *Best Laid Schemes: The Psychology of Emotion* (Cambridge: Cambridge University Press, 1992).

54. Rosalind Piccard, *Affective Computing* (Cambridge: MIT Press, 1997), 136.

55. Gerald W. Edelman, *Bright Air, Brilliant Fire: On the Matter of the Mind* (New York: Basic Books, 1992).

56. John Puddefoot, *God and the Mind Machine: Computers, Artificial Intelligence, and the Human Soul* (London: SPCK, 1996), 92.

57. Francis Crick, *The Astonishing Hypothesis: The Scientific Search for the Soul* (New York: Charles Scribner's Sons, 1994), 3.

58. Ibid., 252.

59. Dennett, *Consciousness Explained*.

60. Daniel C. Dennett, *Darwin's Dangerous Idea: Evolution and the Meaning of Life* (New York: Simon & Schuster, 1995), 81–83.

61. Thomas Nagel, *The View from Nowhere* (New York: Oxford University Press, 1986).

62. Colin McGinn, *The Problem of Consciousness* (Cambridge: Blackwell's, 1991).

63. Owen Flanagan, *Consciousness Reconsidered* (Cambridge: MIT Press, 1992).

64. David J. Chalmers, *The Conscious Mind: In Search of a Fundamental Theory* (New York: Oxford University Press, 1996), 305.

65. Ibid., 300.

66. Lynne Rudder Baker, *Explaining Attitudes: A Practical Approach to Mind* (Cambridge: Cambridge University Press, 1995).

67. The classic source is Alfred North Whitehead, *Process and Reality* (New York: Macmillan, 1929); for an introductory account, see John B. Cobb Jr. and David Ray Griffin, *Process Theology: An Introduction* (Philadelphia: Westminster Press, 1976).

68. Charles Hartshorne, "The Compound Individual," in *Philosophical Essays for Alfred North Whitehead*, F. S. C. Northrup, ed. (New York: Russell & Russell, 1967).

69. David Ray Griffin, "Some Whiteheadian Comments," in *Mind in Nature: Essays on the Interface of Science and Philosophy*, John B. Cobb Jr. and David Ray Griffin, eds. (Washington D.C.: University Press of America, 1977).

70. David Ray Griffin, *Unsnarling the World Knot: Consciousness, Freedom, and the Mind-Body Problem* (Berkeley and Los Angeles: University of California Press, 1998).

71. Alfred North Whitehead, *Adventures of Ideas* (New York: Macmillan, 1933), 226.

72. Alfred North Whitehead, *Process and Reality*, corrected ed., David Ray Griffin and Donald W. Sherburne, eds. (New York: Free Press, 1978), 162.

73. Charles Hartshorne, *Reality as Social Process* (Glencoe, Ill.: Free Press, 1953), chap. 1; *idem, The Logic of Perfection* (LaSalle, Ill.: Open Court, 1962), chap. 7.

74. Barbour, *Religion and Science*, 290.

75. Joseph A. Bracken, S.J., "Revising Process Metaphysics in Response to Ian Barbour's Critique," *Zygon* 33 (1998): 407.

76. Ibid, 408.

77. See also Frank Kirkpatrick, "Process or Agent: Two Models for Self and God," in *Philosophy of Religion and Theology*, David Ray Griffin, ed. (Chambersburg, Pa.: American Academy of Religion, 1971); Paul Sponheim, *Faith and Process: The Significance of Process Thought for Christian Thought* (Minneapolis: Augsburg, 1979), 90–98.

78. See chapters by Philip Clayton and Arthur Peacocke in *Neuroscience and the Person: Scientific Perspectives on Divine Action,* ed. Robert John Russell, Nancey Murphy, Theo C. Meyering, and Michael A. Arbib (Vatican: Vatican Observatory; Berkeley, Calif.: Center for Theology and the Natural Sciences, 1999).

79. See Barbour, *Religion and Science*, 289–93.

Chapter 5: God and Nature: A Process View

1. Ian G. Barbour, *Myths, Models and Paradigms: A Comparative Study in Science and Religion* (New York: Harper & Row, 1974), chaps. 3–5.

2. G. W. H. Lampe, *God as Spirit* (Oxford: Clarendon Press, 1977).

3. Étienne Gilson, *The Christian Philosophy of Thomas Aquinas* (New York: Random House, 1956).

4. Dante Alighieri, *The Paradiso,* trans. John Ciardi (New York: New American Library, 1970), canto 33.

5. See essays by George F. R. Ellis, John Polkinghorne, and Arthur Peacocke in *Chaos and Complexity: Scientific Perspectives on Divine Action,* ed. Robert John Russell, Nancey Murphy, and Arthur Peacocke (Vatican: Vatican Observatory; Berkeley, Calif.: Center for Theology and the Natural Sciences, 1995). Ellis and Peacocke also have essays in *Evolutionary and Molecular Biology: Scientific Perspectives on Divine Action,* ed. Robert John Russell, William R. Stoeger, and Francisco J. Ayala (Vatican: Vatican Observatory; Berkeley, Calif.: Center for Theology and Natural Sciences, 1998).

6. Michael Welker, "What Is Creation? Rereading Genesis 1 and 2," *Theology Today* 47 (April 1991): 56–70.

7. Karl Barth, *Church Dogmatics* (Edinburgh: T & T Clark, 1958) 3/3: 49, 94, 106, 133, 148, etc.; Austin Farrer, *Faith and Speculation* (London: Adam and Charles Black, 1967), chaps. 4 and 10.

8. Donald R. Griffin, *Animal Minds: Beyond Cognition to Consciousness* (Chicago: University of Chicago Press, 2001).

9. Holmes Rolston III, *Science and Religion: A Critical Survey* (Philadelphia: Temple University Press, 1987), 137–38.

10. Ibid., chap. 3.

11. John Hick, *Evil and the Love of God* (San Francisco: Harper & Row, 1966).

12. Ted Peters, *Playing God: Genetic Determinism or Human Freedom?* (New York and London: Routledge, 1997).

13. E. L. Mascall, *He Who Is: A Study in Traditional Theism* (London: Longman's Green and Co., 1945); Richard Creel, *Divine Impassibility: An Essay in Philosophical Theology* (Cambridge: Cambridge University Press, 1986).

14. John Polkinghorne, *The Faith of a Physicist* (Princeton: Princeton University Press, 1994), 83–85.

15. W. H. Vanstone, *Love's Endeavor, Love's Expense* (London: Dartmon, Longman, and Todd, 1977), 120.

16. Paul S. Fiddes, *The Creative Suffering of God* (Oxford: Clarendon Press, 1988).

17. Rosemary Radford Ruether, *Sexism and God-Talk: Toward a Feminist Theology* (Boston: Beacon Press, 1983).

18. Sallie McFague, *Models of God for an Ecological, Nuclear Age* (Philadelphia: Fortress Press, 1987).

19. Elizabeth A. Johnson, *She Who Is: The Mystery of God in Feminist Theological Discourse* (New York: Crossroad Press, 1992).

20. Joanne Carlson Brown and Rebecca Parker, "For God So Loved the World?" in *Christianity, Patriarchy, and Abuse: A Feminist Critique,* ed. Joanne Carlson Brown and Carole R. Bohn (New York: Pilgrim Press, 1989).

21. Alfred North Whitehead, *Process and Reality* (New York: Macmillan, 1929), 352.

22. See John B. Cobb Jr. and David Ray Griffin, *Process Theology: An Introduction* (Philadelphia: Westminster Press, 1976).

23. Charles Hartshorne, *The Divine Relativity* (New Haven: Yale University Press, 1948).

24. David Ray Griffin, *Unsnarling the World Knot: Consciousness, Freedom, and the Mind/Body Problem* (Berkeley and Los Angeles: University of California Press, 1998).

25. Charles Hartshorne, *Omnipotence and Other Theological Mistakes* (Albany: State University of New York Press, 1984), 25.

26. Charles Hartshorne, *Reality as Social Process* (Glencoe, Ill.: Free Press, 1953).

27. Daniel Day Williams, "How Does God Act? An Essay in Whitehead's Metaphysics," in *Process and Divinity,* ed. W. L. Reese and E. Freeman (LaSalle, Ill.: Open Court, 1964), 177.

28. Daniel Day Williams, *The Spirit and the Forms of Love* (New York: Harper & Row, 1968), 185. See also Daniel Day Williams, "The Vulnerable and the Invulnerable God," *Christianity and Crisis* 22 (March 6, 1962): 27–30. On Williams's views, see Warren McWilliams, *The Passion of God: Divine Suffering in Contemporary Protestant Thought* (Macon, Ga.: Mercer University Press, 1985), chap. 6.

29. Daniel Day Williams, "Deity, Monarchy, and Metaphysics: Whitehead's Critique of the Theological Tradition," in *The Relevance of Whitehead,* ed. I. Leclerc (New York: Macmillan, 1961).

30. Daniel Day Williams, "Suffering and Being in Empirical Theology," in *The Future of Empirical Theology,* ed. Bernard Meland (Chicago: University of Chicago Press, 1969), 191.

31. Anna Case-Winter, *God's Power: Traditional Understanding and Contemporary Challenges* (Louisville: Westminster John Knox, 1990).

32. Sheila Greeve Davaney, ed., *Feminism and Process Thought* (New York and Toronto: Edwin Mellen Press, 1981); Sallie McFague, *The Body of God: An Ecological Theology* (Minneapolis: Fortress Press, 1993).

33. Alfred North Whitehead, *Process and Reality,* corrected ed., David Ray Griffin and Donald W. Sherburne, eds. (New York: Free Press, 1978), 91.

34. Charles Hartshorne, *Man's Vision of God* (Chicago: Willet Clark, 1941), 230–34; Cobb and Griffin, *Process Theology,* 64–67; Lewis Ford, "An Alternative to *Creatio ex Nihilo,*" *Religious Studies* 19 (1983): 205–13.

35. Andre Linde, "The Self-Reproducing Universe," *Scientific American* 271 (November 1994): 48–55; Alan Guth, *The Inflationary Universe* (Reading, Mass.: Addison-Wesley, 1997); John Gribbin, *In the Beginning* (Boston: Little Brown, 1993).

36. Rem Edwards, "How Process Theology Can Affirm Creation *ex Nihilo,*" *Process Studies* 29 (2000): 77–96.

37. Claus Westerman, *Beginning and End in the Bible* (Philadelphia: Fortress Press, 1972).

38. David Ray Griffin, *God, Power, and Evil: A Process Theodicy* (Philadelphia: Westminster Press, 1976); also his "Creation Out of Chaos and the Problem of Evil," in *Encountering Evil: Live Options in Theodicy,* ed. Stephen Davis (Atlanta: John Knox, 1988).

39. See Cobb and Griffin, *Process Theology,* chap. 7.

40. John B. Cobb Jr., "What Is the Future? A Process Perspective," in *Hope and the Future,* ed. Ewart Cousins (Philadelphia: Fortress Press, 1972).

41. Marjorie Hewett Suchocki, *The End of Evil: Process Eschatology in Historical Context* (Albany: State University of New York Press, 1988), chap. 5.

42. Marjorie Hewett Suchocki, *God, Christ, Church: A Practical Guide to Process Theology* (New York: Crossroad, 1982).

Chapter 6: Theology, Ethics, and the Environment

1. See Lester Brown et al., *State of the World 2001* (New York: Norton, 2001); World Resources Institute, *World Resources, 2000–2001* (New York: Basic Books, 2000); Population Reference Bureau Website, "2001 World Population Data," September 2001.

2. Intergovernmental Panel on Climate Change, *Climate Change: The Scientific Basis* (Cambridge: Cambridge University Press, 2001).

3. Ian G. Barbour, *Technology, Environment, and Human Values* (New York: Praeger, 1980), chaps. 8 and 9; also *idem, Ethics in an Age of Technology,* Gifford Lectures vol. 2 (San Francisco: HarperSanFrancisco, 1993), chap. 8.

4. Lynn White, "The Historical Roots of Our Ecologic Crisis," reprinted, with articles by critics and White's response to them, in Ian G. Barbour, ed., *Western Man and Environmental Ethics* (Reading, Mass.: Addison-Wesley, 1973).

5. For example, Rosemary Radford Ruether, *Gaia and God: An Ecofeminist Theology of Earth Healing* (San Francisco: HarperSanFrancisco, 1992); Carol Adams, ed., *Ecofeminism and the Sacred* (New York: Continuum, 1993); Mary Heather MacKinnon and Moni M. McIntyre, eds., *Readings in Ecology and Feminist Theology* (Kansas City: Sheed and Ward, 1995).

6. Max Oelschlaeger, *Caring for the Earth: An Ecumenical Approach to the Environmental Crisis* (New Haven: Yale University Press, 1994).

7. Recent volumes covering a range of perspectives on Christian environmentalism include Dieter T. Hessel and Rosemary Radford Ruether, eds., *Christianity and Ecology: Seeking the Well-Being of Earth and Humans* (Cambridge: Harvard University Press, 2000); and David Hallman, ed., *Ecotheology: Voices from North and South* (Maryknoll, N.Y.: Orbis, 1994).

8. Douglas John Hall, *Imaging God: Dominion as Stewardship* (Grand Rapids, Mich.: Eerdmans, 1986); Peter DeVos, ed., *Earthkeeping in the Nineties* (Grand Rapids, Mich.: Eerdmans, 1991).

9. James A. Nash, *Loving Nature: Ecological Integrity and Christian Responsibility* (Nashville: Abingdon Press, 1991); see also Larry L. Rasmussen, *Earth Community, Earth Ethics* (Maryknoll, N.Y.: Orbis, 1996).

10. G. W. H. Lampe, *God as Spirit* (Oxford: Clarendon Press, 1977); Alasdair Heron, *The Holy Spirit* (Philadelphia: Westminister Press, 1987); Mark I. Wallace, *Fragments of the Spirit: Nature, Violence, and the Renewal of Creation* (New York: Continuum, 1996).

11. George H. Kehm, "The New Story: Redemption as Fulfillment of Creation," in *After Nature's Revolt: Eco-Justice and Theology*, Dieter T. Hessel, ed. (Minneapolis: Fortress Press, 1992).

12. Paulos Gregarios, "New Testament Foundations for Understanding the Creation," in *Tending the Garden*, ed. Wesley Granberg-Michaelson (Grand Rapids, Mich.: Eerdmans, 1987).

13. Metropolitan John of Pergamon (John Zizoulos), "Preserving God's Creation," in *Christianity and Ecology*, ed. Elizabeth Breuilly and Martin Palmer (London and New York: Caswell Publishers, 1992).

14. John Habgood, "A Sacramental Approach to Environmental Issues," in *Liberating Life: Contemporary Approaches to Ecological Theology*, Charles Birch, William Eakin, and Jay McDaniel, eds. (Maryknoll, N.Y.: Orbis, 1990).

15. Pierre Teilhard de Chardin, *The Divine Milieu* (New York: Harper & Row, 1960).

16. Matthew Fox, *The Coming of the Cosmic Christ: The Healing of Mother Earth and the Birth of a Global Renaissance* (San Francisco: Harper & Row, 1988); see also Brian Swimme and Thomas Berry, *Universe Story* (San Francisco: HarperSanFrancisco, 1992).

17. See Ian G. Barbour, *Religion and Science: Historical and Contemporary Issues* (San Francisco: HarperSanFrancisco, 1997), chap. 10.

18. George Tinker, "Creation as Kin: An American Indian View," in *After Nature's Revolt*, Hessel, ed.; John A. Grim, "Native American Worldviews and Ecology," in *Worldviews and Ecology*, Mary Evelyn Tucker and John A. Grim, eds. (Maryknoll, N.Y.: Orbis, 1994).

19. Shepard Krech III, *The Ecological Indian: Myth and History* (New York: Norwich, 1999).

20. Ursula Goodenough, *The Sacred Depths of Nature* (New York: Oxford University Press, 1998).

21. John B. Cobb Jr. and David Ray Griffin, *Process Theology: An Introduction* (Philadelphia: Westminster Press, 1976); see also Barbour, *Religion and Science*, chap. 11.

22. Jay McDaniel, *Of God and Pelicans: A Theology of Reverence for Life* (Louisville: Westminster John Knox, 1989).

23. Presbyterian Eco-Justice Task Force, *Keeping and Healing the Creation* (Louisville: Presbyterian Church USA, 1989); Environmental Task Force, Evangelical Lutheran Church in America, *Caring for Creation* (Minneapolis: ELCA, 1991); U.S. Conference of Catholic Bishops, "Renewing the Earth," *Origins* 21 (1991): 425–32.

24. Wesley Granberg-Michaelson, *Redeeming the Creation: The Rio Earth Summit—Challenges for the Churches* (Geneva: World Council of Churches, 1992); World Council of Churches Study Project, *Climate Change and the Quest for Sustainable Societies* (Geneva: World Council of Churches, 1998).

25. Alan During, *How Much Is Enough? The Consumer Society and the Future of the Earth* (New York: Norton, 1992); Paul Wachtel, *The Poverty of Affluence: A Psychological Portrait of the American Way of Life* (Philadelphia: Free Press, 1983); Michael Argyle, *The Psychology of Happiness* (New York: Methuen, 1987).

26. James Nash, "Toward the Revival and Reform of the Subversive Virtue: Frugality," *Annual of the Society of Christian Ethics* (1995): 137–160; David Shi, *The Simple Life: Plain Living and High Thinking in American Culture* (New York: Oxford University Press, 1985); Rodney Clapp, ed., *The Consuming Passion* (Downers Grove, Ill.: InterVarsity Press, 1997).

27. International Conference on Population and Development, *Programme of Action* (New York: United Nations Population Fund, 1994).

28. Susan Power Bratton, *Six Billion and More: Human Population Regulation and Christian Ethics* (Louisville: Westminster John Knox, 1992); James B. Martin-Schramm, *Population Perils and the Churches' Response* (Geneva: World Council of Churches, 1997); Harold Coward and Daniel Maguire, eds., *Visions of a New Earth: Religious Perspectives on Population, Consumption and Ecology* (Albany: State University of New York Press, 1998).

29. Robert D. Bullard, ed., *Confronting Environmental Racism* (Boston: South End Press, 1993); Laura Westra and Peter Wenz, eds., *Faces of Environmental Racism: Confronting Issues of Global Justice* (Lanham, Md.: Rowman and Littlefield, 1995).

30. Barbour, *Ethics in an Age of Technology*, chaps. 2 and 3.

31. Lester Brown, Christopher Flavin, and Sandra Postel, *Saving the Planet: How to Shape an Environmentally Sustainable Global Economy* (New York: Norton, 1991).

32. United Nations Development Programme, *Human Development Report* (New York: Oxford University Press, 1998).

33. Hilary French, *Vanishing Borders: Protecting the Planet in an Age of Globalization* (New York: Norton, 2000).

34. Dani Rodrik, *Has Integration Gone Too Far?* (Washington, D.C.: Institute for International Economics, 1997); Sarah Anderson and John Cavanaugh, *A Field Guide to the Global Economy* (New York: New Press, 2000).

35. William Greider, *One World, Ready or Not: The Manic Logic of Global Capitalism* (New York: Simon & Schuster, 1997); James M. Mittelman, *The Globalization Syndrome* (Princeton: Princeton University Press, 2000).

36. Thomas L. Friedman, *The Lexus and the Olive Tree: Understanding Globalization*, expanded ed. (New York: Random House, 2000).

Index of Authors

Gehring, Walter, 144 n.14
Gergen, K. J., 150 n.8
Gilbert, Walter, 59, 148 n.45
Gilson, Étienne, 153 n.3
Gleick, James, 21, 144 n.21, 145 n.26
Goldberg, Michael, 151 n.42
Goodall, Jane, 42–43, 147 n.9
Goodenough, Ursula, 156 n.20
Goodwin, Brian, 15, 144 n.15
Gould, Stephen Jay, 12–13, 14, 143
    nn.5–6
Granberg-Michaelson, Wesley, 156
    n.12, 157 n.24
Grant, Frederick C., 151 n.35
Green, Joel B., 79, 151 n.29
Gregarios, Paulos, 126, 156 n.12
Greider, William, 157 n.35
Gribbin, John, 155 n.35
Griffin, David Ray, 6, 34, 37, 78, 116,
    146 nn.50–52, 150 n.18, 152
    nn.67–70, 154 n.8, 153 n.72, 153
    n.77, 154 n.22, 154 n.24, 155
    nn.33–34, 155 nn.38–39, 156 n.21
Grim, John A., 156 n.18
Guth, Alan, 155 n.35

Habgood, John, 156 n.14
Haight, Roger S., 56, 148 n.38
Halder, George, 144 n.14
Hall, Douglas John, 156 n.8
Hallie, Philip Paul, 148 n.42
Hallman, David, 156 n.7
Hammer, Dean, 148 n.48
Harré, Rom, 150 n.8
Hartshorne, Charles, 32, 37, 95, 97,
    111, 112, 113, 146 n.47, 152 n.68,
    153 n.73, 154 n.23, 154 nn.25–26,
    155 n.34
Hawking, Stephen, 29
Hefner, Philip, 52, 148 n.30
Heidegger, Martin, 85
Heron, Alisdair, 146 n.53, 156 n.10
Hessel, Dieter T., 156 n.7, 156 n.11,
    156 n.18
Hick, John, 106, 154 n.11
Hildegard of Bingen, 127
Ho, Mae-Won, 15, 144 n.15, 144 n.25
Hodgson, Peter, 151 n.36

Holland, Suzanne, 149 n.55
Holte, John, 144 n.21
Hood, Leroy, 148 n.45
Hoyle, Fred, 144 n.17
Hutchingson, James, 32, 146 n.48
Huxley, Julian, 11, 47

Irenaeus, St., 106
Isaiah, 108, 136
Izard, Carroll, 150 n.5

Jacobsen, C., 147 n.21
James, William, 73, 91, 97–98, 150 n.6
Jaroff, L., 148 n.44
Jaspers, Karl, 49, 147 n.23
Jeeves, Malcolm A., 83, 151 n.44
Jentzen, Grace, 146 n.41
Jesus, 4, 8, 30, 34, 37, 49, 52, 53–57,
    103, 108–111, 113, 114, 116, 117,
    118, 125, 126, 136
John (biblical author), 116
Johnson, Elizabeth A., 110, 154 n.19
Joyce, James, 91
Julian of Norwich, 127

Kant, Immanuel, 38
Kauffman, Stuart, 14, 16, 17–18, 144
    n.12, 144 n.19
Keenan, James, 151 n.37
Kehm, George H., 156 n.11
Kellert, Stephen H., 19, 144 n.22
Kelsey, David, 151 n.36
Kevles, Daniel J., 148 n.45
King, Robert, 151 n.36
Kirkpatrick, Frank, 153 n.77
Kramer, Peter R., 72, 149 n.3
Krech, Shepard III, 157 n.19
Kuhn, Thomas J., 15, 144 n.16

Lacayo, Richard, 149 n.54
Lakatos, Imre, 16, 144 n.16
Lamark, Jean Baptiste, 11, 13
Lampe, G. W. H., 55–56, 146 n.53,
    148 n.37, 153 n.2, 156 n.10
Lazarus, Richard, 150 n.7
Lebacqz, Karen, 149 n.55
LeDoux, Joseph, 73–74, 150 n.9
Leopold, Aldo, 128

Index of Subjects

complexity. *See* self-organization
computational brain, 83–85
computers
  consciousness in, 88–90
  emotions in, 87–88
  socialization of, 86–88
conflict thesis, 1
consciousness, 16, 34, 44, 86, 93–94,
    95, 96–97, 98, 99, 111–12,
    131
  as emergent, 92
  in computers, 88–90
  construction of self and, 78–79,
    129
  degrees of, 78
  eliminative materialism and,
    90–91
  evolution of, 77–78, 106
  irreducibility of, 91–92, 93
  unconscious information process-
    ing, 77
consumption, 133–34, 137
context of interpretation, 24, 84
contextualism, 98, 136
cooperation, 41, 45, 52, 105
cosmology, 29, 50, 114–16
cosmos, 3, 35
creation, 4, 36, 38, 49–50, 81, 105,
    106, 113, 115–16, 122, 123,
    124, 125
  continuing, 38, 56, 70, 99, 126,
    131
creativity, 26, 108, 110, 112, 115, 129
criminal behavior, 61
cross, the, 8, 17, 35, 55, 108–9, 118
cultural evolution, 42, 44, 47
culture, 42, 44–46, 47, 48, 75–76
  episodic, 45
  mythic, 45

Darwinism, 1–2, 7, 41, 72
  beyond, 14–16
  expansion of, 12–14
death, 4, 26, 44, 46, 48, 51, 55, 80, 81,
    89, 106, 108, 109, 110, 116,
    117–18
deism, 3, 26

design, 3, 25–27, 35
determinism,
  physical, 11, 104
  genetic, 59-70, 107
  divine, 27, 103, 112
developing nations, 137–39
dialogue thesis, 1–2
dipolar monism, 94–96, 100
directionality of evolution, 16, 17
discrimination, 135
distributed patterns, 21, 86
divine intervention, 25, 27, 104
divine sovereignty. *See* omnipotence
divine transcendence, 9, 27, 34, 104,
    115, 121, 128, 131–32
DNA. *See* molecular biology
dual-aspect theory, 91–92, 93
dualism (body/soul, mind/matter),
    6, 8, 37, 52, 65, 71, 79–80, 82,
    83, 84, 90, 91, 96, 98, 99, 111,
    112, 126, 131
  beyond, 128–29

ecology, 9, 10, 22, 32, 130, 132–133
embodiment, 71–72, 85–86, 96
  robots and, 85–86
embryo, status of, 64
embryology, 15
emergence, 6, 60, 97, 98–99, 100
  first-order, 22
  second-order, 22–23
  third-order, 23
emotions, 72–74, 80–81, 82, 96–97,
    106
  in body-response perspective, 73
  in cognitive perspective, 73
  in computers, 87–88
  in evolutionary perspective, 72–73
  in neural perspective, 73–74
  in social perspective, 73, 75
environment, 38, 130
  science and, 38, 119–20, 130
  social justice and, 132–40
  stewardship of, 121, 124, 132–33
  theology and, 121–24
epistemological reduction, 20
epistemology, 5

eschatology, 116-17
ethics, 38, 119–24, 129–30, 132–40.
    See also social justice
eugenics, 67–68
evil, 8, 27, 48, 52, 53, 68, 81, 105–8,
    113, 116–17, 129
evolution, 3–4, 7, 8, 11–38, 39, 51, 54,
    92, 99, 105–6, 123, 129–30.
    See also Human evolution
evolutionary psychology, 40–41
ex nihilo creation, 115–116
experience, 34, 93–94, 95–96, 131

Fall, the, 50
family, 58, 69
feminist thought, 59, 82, 109–11, 114,
    121–22
fetus, 64
fine-tuning of early universe, 2-3
formalist computer theory, 84
freedom, human, 8, 27, 28, 46, 54,
    57, 59, 62, 105–8, 112
free-process defense, 108

Genesis, 4, 49, 50, 51, 102, 105, 121,
    124–25, 128
genetic(s), 8, 11, 13, 15, 16, 18,
    24–25, 34, 40, 41, 42, 52
    assimilation, 14–15
    behavioral, 61–62
    determinism, 59–70, 107
    drift, 18
    eugenics, 67–68
    germ-line therapy, 66–67
    modification, 66–68
    selection of desirable genes, 67
    single-gene defects , 60–61
    somatic cell therapy, 66
global justice, 137–38
global warming, 120
globalization, 9, 138–40
gnosticism, 81, 112
God
    images of, 49–50, 68–69, 102, 121,
        128
    as impassable, 103
    persuasion *vs.* coercion, 111

power of, 6, 8, 9, 34, 37, 70, 101,
    105, 108, 112–14
    purposeful, 76
    theism *vs.* Deism , 3
God's action
    in nature, 25–31, 105, 125–28
    in process theology, 31–39
God's self-limitation (*kenosis*), 8, 37,
    101, 104–11, 112–17
Greek thought, 4, 38, 49, 80, 81, 84,
    102, 103, 117, 121, 126, 128
guilt, 50, 53, 73, 88

hierarchical organization, 15
hierarchy theory, 17
Hinduism, 79
holism (wholes and parts), 6, 13, 14,
    21, 22, 23, 28, 29, 32, 48, 51,
    71, 78, 97, 113, 129
Homo erectus, 39, 46
    mimetic culture of, 46
Homo sapiens, 39
human (beings), 96, 99
    developmental view of, 65–66
    dignity, 69, 89
    kinship with other creatures, 50,
        129-30
    morality of, 40–42, 43
    uniqueness of, 45, 50, 99
human evolution, 39–49
human genome, 59–62

imago Dei, 50, 128
immanence, 9, 34, 35, 36, 54, 114,
    127, 128, 132
immortality, 81, 117–118
in vitro fertilization, 64, 67
independence thesis, 1
indeterminacy, 18–19, 27–28, 32, 35
information, 71–72
    bits of, 23
    communication of, 23–25, 30–31,
        32, 35, 97
    cultural, 42
    historically acquired, 24–25
    states, 93
    theory, 23

integration thesis, 2, 7
intelligence, 43, 46, 84
interdependence, 75, 86, 96, 99, 130
interiority, 33–34, 95
internal drives, 13
invertebrates, 95
Islam, 49

Jesus, 4, 8, 30, 34, 36, 37, 49, 52, 103,
     113, 125, 126, 127, 136
    creedal formulas, 54
    the cross, suffering and, 108–11
    historical and relational cate-
        gories, 54
    human and divine in, 53–56
Judaism, 4, 49, 50, 51, 53, 58, 79, 80,
     81, 102–3, 108, 115, 117, 125,
     136
justice. See social justice

kenosis, 108. See also God's self–limita-
    tion

language, 43-44, 45, 75-76, 84
large-scale effects, 19, 27
learning, 85–86, 93
levels, 15, 17, 20
    hierarchy of, 97, 111
    of selection, 41
    reduction between, 20-21
life, 3, 21, 31, 33, 48, 80
    individual and social, 84
limbic system, 76
linguistic analysis, 43, 44–46, 75, 83,
     90–91, 93, 96
    as context-dependent, 84
    two-languages approach, 83
Logos. See Word, divine
love, 34–35, 55–57, 69, 80, 127
    call to, 55–57
    divine, 106, 107, 110, 111, 112,
      113, 125
    forms of, 55–56
    self-sacrificial, 109, 110, 117
    unconditional, 69–70

materialism, 4–5, 8, 71, 90–91, 111,
    131
medieval thought, 4, 26, 38, 54, 58,
    65, 81–82, 101, 103–4, 125
memory, 21, 23, 72, 75, 76, 88, 92, 93,
    95, 98
mental abilities/activities, 78, 93, 99,
    111–12
metacontrast, 77
metaphysical pluralism, 94
metaphysics, 5, 99, 127–28, 130
    generality of metaphysical cate-
      gories, 99
    necessity, 112–13
methodological reduction, 20
mind, 34, 82, 89, 95, 96, 99
models, 16, 102
modern synthesis, 11, 12, 14
molecular biology, 6, 12, 13, 16, 21,
    24, 39, 59–62, 66, 90, 130
monism, 94–96, 98, 111
    dipolar, 94–96, 100
    emergent, 98–99
moral choice, 107–108
morality, 26, 40–42, 43, 106–7, 110
myths, 45, 47–48, 68, 76

natural selection, 11, 12, 13, 15, 16,
    42
natural theology, 2–3, 25
nature, 48, 121, 122
    artificial intelligence and, 90–94
    creativity vs. freedom in, 108
    God's action in, 25–31, 105,
      124–28
    humanity and, 128–32
    integrity of, 104–5
    theology, environment and,
      121–24
    whole-part relationships in, 28
Neanderthals, 40, 46
neocortex, 76
network properties, 21–22
neural paths, 74, 88, 90, 92
New Testament, 51, 79, 80, 102, 116

Newtonian physics, 5, 11, 14, 16
nonreductive naturalism, 92

objectivity, 41
Old Testament, 49, 51, 79
omnipotence, 6, 8, 9, 37, 101, 103,
     105, 108, 112–13
omniscience, 101, 108, 112
ontological continuity, 99
ontological reduction, 20–21, 22
order, 17-18, 23-24, 106
organizational pluralism, 94–96, 98,
     100
original sin, *see* sin; Fall, the

panadaptationsim, 13
panexperientalism, 36–37, 95, 111
panpsychism, 93, 95, 111
paradigm shift, 15–16
parallel distributed processing
     (PDP), 85
patriarchal models, 109–11, 121, 125
patterns, 23-24
     distributed, 21
     of events, 30
perception, 71–72, 84
     as context-dependent, 84
physics, 5, 11, 16, 18–19, 84, 93–94.
          See also Newtonian physics;
          quantum physics
planets, 56–57
plants, 95
pluralism, 94–96, 98, 100, 111
political accountability, 138–39
population, 11, 120, 133–35
predestination, 108, 112
primary cause, 26
probability, 11, 18, 27, 104
process philosophy, 2, 6–7, 31–32,
          36–37, 38, 94–100, 109
process theology, 8–9, 34–36, 37, 101,
          108, 111–18, 131–32
Protestantism, 81, 103, 122–23, 125,
          132, 135
psychology, 92, 93, 94
     evolutionary, 40–41

punctuated equilibrium, 12–13

quantum physics, 3, 18–19, 27-28, 35,
     104
     quantum vacuum fluctuations,
          115

readiness potential, 77
reconciliation, 55, 57, 108
redemption, 4, 36, 50, 52, 56, 57, 101,
          113, 118, 122, 125, 126–27,
          128
reductionism, 5, 6, 8, 14, 20–21, 21,
          28, 32, 60.90–91, 92, 129
relationality, 55, 81, 97, 98, 131
religious experience, 48–49, 123,
          127–28, 130
repentance, 125
resurrection, 35, 80, 117–18
revelation, 4, 35, 54
ritual, 45, 47, 48, 76
robotics, 85–90. *See also* computers

sacredness of nature, 127–128
selection, 115
     of desirable genes, 67
     on many levels, 12, 41
self, 88, 96, 97, 103, 117. *See also*
          social self
     causal efficacy of, 93
     construction of, 78–79, 92–93,
          97–98, 129
     embodied, 79–80
     intentional stance of, 91
     as linguistic fiction, 90–91, 93
     narrative, 82, 93
     neuroscience and, 71–79
     in theology, 79–83
self-awareness, 44, 53, 78, 89
self-determination, 44–45, 62, 115
self-interest, 41–42, 69, 130
self-organization (complexity),
          14–15, 16–18, 25–27, 32, 35
self-sacrifice, 40, 58, 110
sentience, 77, 105, 106

sign language, 43
sin, 4, 55, 80, 110, 126–127
   as estrangement, 51, 128–29
   evolutionary interpretation of, 52
   original, 51–53, 68, 69, 127
   social patterns of, 52
   sociobiology and, 52–53
social justice, 52, 69, 120, 132-40
social self, 74–76, 80–81, 82, 96,
   128–29
   cultural symbol systems and,
      75–76
   language and, 76
   memory, narrative construction
      and, 75
   social interaction of, 74–75
socialization, 86-88, 89, 93, 112
sociobiology, 40–42, 43, 52–53, 57,
   58, 73
sociology, 94
soul , 65, 74, 80, 81, 82, 106, 127, 129.
   See also self.
space, 56-57, 115
Spirit (Holy Spirit), 9, 36, 38, 55–56,
   56, 57, 74, 102–3, 109, 110,
   125–26, 127, 128
stem cells, 63–64, 65
   therapeutic *vs.* reproductive uses,
      64
stewardship of nature, 121, 124,
   132–133
structuralism, 15
subjectivity, 33, 36, 41, 98–100, 117
substrate neutrality, 84
suffering, 8, 26, 27, 35, 51, 57, 101,
   105–8, 109, 110, 111, 113–14,
   117–18, 131, 136
sustainability, 132–133

Symbolic Artificial Intelligence,
   83–85
symbolic representation, 44–46, 96,
   128
systemic properties, 17

Tao Te Ching, 49
technology, 132, 135-36, 139
theism, 3, 5, 25, 104, 111
theology, 4. *See also* process theology
   environment and, 82, 121–24,
      132–34
   genetics and, 68–70
   human nature in, 49–59
   medieval, 81–82
   narrative, 82–83
   natural, 2–3, 25
   self in, 79–83
   two-language approach, 83, 96
thermodynamics, 14, 19, 27, 106
Thomism (neo-Thomism), 26, 105,
   108
time, 94–95, 103, 108, 115
top-down causation, 20–23, 28–30,
   32, 35, 60, 97, 105, 111
transcendence. *See* divine transcendence; God
Turing test, 84
two-aspect theory, 92–94, 96

unpredictability, 18-19, 56-57

values, status of, 41
vertebrates, 95

wholes and parts. *See* holism
Word, divine, 31, 102
world as God's body, 29–30, 35, 102